GRADE TRANSFORMER FOR THE MODERN STUDENT

3RD AND 4TH GRADE EDITION

BARBARA DIANIS MA ED

Copyright © 2021 Barbara Dianis MA ED

All rights reserved. No part of this publication in print or in electronic format may be reproduced, stored in a retrieval system, or transmitted in any form or by any means, electronic, mechanical, photocopying, recording, or otherwise without the prior written permission of the publisher.

The scanning, uploading, and distribution of this book without permission is a theft of the author's intellectual property. Thank you for your support of the author's rights.

Design and distribution by Bublish, Inc.

ISBN: (eBook)
ISBN: (paperback)

Contents

Introduction v

August
Learning For An Academically Successful Start
Of The New School Year 1

September
Learning Strategies To Help Children Begin
The School Year Academically Strong 9

October
Learning Ideas And Proven Strategies For Grade Improvement 19

November
Learning Strategies To Help Children Improve Their Grades 27

December
Learning Strategies For To Help Elevate Grades 37

January
Scholastic Tips To Help Start The New Year Off Strong 47

February
Learning Strategies To Help Bring Academic Achievement 55

March
Academic Guidance For Scholastic Achievement 65

April
Learning Strategies To Promote Success In School 73

May
Learning Strategies To Help Students Finish The School Year
Academically Successful 83

June
Summer Brain Drain Prevention 91

July
Summer Fun Learning 103

Bibliography 111

Glossary of Terms 113

About the Author 115

Introduction

Today's parents and elementary students weekly open class grades online, hoping to see satisfactory to above-average grades. Unfortunately, the grades staring back at them are low average, below average, or to everyone's horror, failing ones. Parents and students find themselves wondering what can transform this devastating learning situation into academic success.

Parents and elementary school students often want to handle academic struggles confidentially. Others wish only a handful of people are made aware that a class or classes have become overwhelming, and earning high test grades and or above-average grades may seem improbable. Struggling students need help **now**! They need proven educational solutions and methods to help transform their low grades and learn how to catch up in their fundamental skills and classes **as fast as possible**.

Numerous struggling students' parents cannot spend hundreds to thousands of dollars to help their child overcome their learning obstacles. For the first time, the proven methods used to transform the academic performance of struggling students into scholastic success stories are now available in ***Grade Transformer for the Modern Student 3*** rd ***and 4*** th ***Grade Edition.*** The book and methods are comparable to having a private learning specialist guiding the student through the academic maze to help them so that they too can transform into **academic winners**.

Introduction

Traditionally once an elementary student begins to fall behind their peers in one or more fundamental subject areas, it can be challenging to maintain one's scholastic competitive edge. As a student's low or below-average grades evolve into a series of substandard grades and classroom performance seems incommensurate with their peers, one's self-esteem can deteriorate toward academic learning. **Grade Transformer for the Modern Student 3rd and 4th Grade Edition** can help restore children's academic self-esteem and provide hope for a brighter educational future.

Whether students' academic issues are directly correlated to Dyslexia, ADD/ADHD, disorganization, poor executive management skills, motivational problems, or a lack of understanding may be the underlining issue of the student's low marks, the methods in this book can help them. The excellent news is step-by-step educational and test-taking solutions can help them reach their true learning potential.

Educational secrets and solutions children apply directly to their current academic curriculum's homework and study time can transform underachieving students into ones with a restored scholastic competitive edge.

The author Barbara Dianis has stood in the shoes of numerous students falling behind in school. She was diagnosed with Dyslexia and began her journey to overcome every learning obstacle she faced. During the years Dianis was being educated, the answers and solutions for academic issues were even fewer than in today's world. Subsequently, Dianis set out to design her own educational methods and study techniques to make herself an academic winner despite having to overcome Dyslexia.

Through her journey to be educated, she discovered educational methods and study techniques that took her from Dyslexic to a member of the prestigious **National Dean's List** for the academic elite. Dianis concluded if she could overcome her learning obstacles, so could other students.

Dianis's journey continued as she became an Educational Specialist who is certified to teach Pre-K-12th students. During the past twenty-one years, Dianis has taught students from all walks of life Pre-K-12th who were experiencing academic difficulties to succeed at learning.

The educational methods and techniques detailed in **Grade Transformer for the Modern Student 3rd and 4th Grade Edition** and **Bool 1 and Book 11 of Don't Count Me Out** are a compilation of years of helping Dyslexic, ADD/ADHD, and Struggling Students become academic winners.

Grade Transformer for the Modern Student

Whether your child needs to improve their grades in one, or more fundamental educational subjects, this book can help transform elementary students into scholastically victorious students. The methods, academic secrets, and study techniques can help create happy, confident, and academically successful students who enjoy learning. Now is the time to help your son or daughter to transform their learning obstacles into academic success.

August

Learning For An Academically Successful Start Of The New School Year

August

The warmer days and the smell of late summer flowers remind children that summer vacation will be over in the following weeks. Soon back to school shopping will be filling children's minds as they plan for the new year. Everywhere one looks are colorful and fantastic-looking school supplies. New school fashion advertisements are beaconing shoppers to back to the stores. Parents want to ensure their children have everything they need to begin another school year. Therefore, zealous conversations about preparing for school are helpful before the new year begins and school supplies are purchased. Third and fourth graders generally enjoy the process of preparing their school supplies for the new year. Back-to-school shopping can be a fun time and productive way to teach organizational skills.

While shopping for school supplies, parents should purchase a small plastic crate or study box for their students to store all of their at-home supplies inside. The supply crate for homework and study time can save students hours and hours of searching for materials that are scattered throughout their homes. In addition, the organized study system can help third and fourth graders learn how to become organized students for their entire school career. Each day, the study supplies crate should be stored in the same place with all the materials placed back into their place. This strategy will help students ensure their supplies are easy to access and not lost in their homes.

★ Designing Study And Homework Schedule Strategies For Success

Third and fourth graders are now entering the school years, where their study and homework load will begin to increase. Therefore, pre-planning homework and study time is a beneficial strategy to help students settle into their new school routine. Prior to the beginning of school, parents and their third or fourth graders should determine a daily homework and study program that will work with their schedule. Then, the homework and study time can be done at different times to fit the student's and family's schedules.

The amount of time third and fourth grades should devote to studying should be determined with their teacher or teachers' input. A permanent study plan should be put in place whether or not they are reading and performing at grade level expectations in their core academic skill areas. If a third or fourth grader is scholastically performing below average, they will benefit from adding an additional twenty minutes per day to remediate their weaker academic skill areas.

Third and fourth graders who are struggling academically in one or more skill areas need to work on remediation at home as well as in school. Whether or not a student is enrolled in a remedial class or working with a tutor, they will benefit from working on remediation at during their daily study time. One consistent mistake parents and students make is, if they are in a remedial class or working with a tutor, they don't continue working on at-home remedial activities. Numerous students don't reach their full academic potential because they believe their remedial class or tutoring will solve their entire educational weaknesses.

However, most students will need to work at home remediating their academic weaknesses to ensure they reach or supersede their previously suggested academic expectations. Students can learn how to overcome their academic issues and excel in school by implementing an at-home remedial program. Educational statistics suggest that third- and fourth-grade students reading below their grade-level standards will continue to struggle in school throughout their school years. Sadly, many will become high school dropouts because they ultimately become unable to keep academic pace with their peers. Caution: relying on the school system remedial program or tutor to solve all of the students' learning issues can result in disappointing results. The good news is students who work on proven remedial methods at home can learn to excel academically.

★ Reading Improvement Strategies To Help Children Succeed In Reading

Third and fourth-grade students are still learning to read and now reading to learn. The focus of reading classes will begin to shift toward decoding multi-syllable words. The grade-level reading materials will contain fewer sight words, as they did in the earlier school years.

In the last few weeks of summer vacation and during the new school year, third and fourth graders should work on learning phonetic spellings. They will benefit from learning them in their adult lives. The phonetic spelling presented in the third and fourth grades can be easily located online.

August

First, ask your third or fourth grader to read orally from reading material that matches their current grade level or just a few months above it. If you are unfamiliar with how to determine what the reading level is of a particular book, then just online or at your local public library for the exact level. Next, while your son or daughter is reading orally to you, make notes over words they are not able to read without decoding or not at all. List the unmastered words on paper or electronic devices that will be easy to access.

Next, keep assessing your son's or daughter's reading level until you have thirty to forty words on the list. The unfamiliar word is an excellent place to begin to determine what phonetic rules should be worked on mastering. Frequently, there will be some consistencies of like phonetic rules in the unmastered words list.

Third and fourth graders benefit from learning word lists they create with you, including the various phonetic rules they need additional instruction to master. The phonetic word lists can be easily created using a dictionary or typing in the phonetic spelling online and copying the words from the results. The word lists may also be printed from the Internet. Then students benefit from learning the phonetic rules in isolation. Learning one at a time phonetic rules can accelerate mastery. Reading over the word lists daily and quoting the phonetic rule and spelling can dramatically assist students in growing in their reading and spelling skills

After the third or fourth grader masters the phonetic rules, they should move on to conquer more of the ones they need extra help learning. Periodically, students should return to the mastered reading lists and review them in order to ensure the information has moved from their short-term memory to their long-term memory.

★ Spelling Improvement For Success

Even in this technological age, the ability to spell words correctly is still an extremely valuable skill. Students who find themselves with long-term spelling issues may find themselves at a disadvantage in the higher-grade levels. They may also find that spelling problems that are never resolved can negatively impact their future careers. Therefore, learning how to spell during the elementary grades can help students enjoy a brighter future throughout their lives.

Although learning to be proficient in the area of spelling can leave third and fourth graders with feelings of dread and boredom. However, learning how to succeed and excel in spelling can be fun instead of humdrum. In addition, as students become better spellers, often their literacy skills improve as an added benefit.

Prior to the beginning of school, third and fourth-grade students should make sure they have been learning to spell the *220 Dolch Sight Words List.* The sight word list can be found online, at the public library, or local public school. Students should take spelling tests over the entire list of 220 words over several days if breaks are needed.

Sight words, which are words that don't follow phonetic rules and are commonly misspelled by students. The troublesome sight words for the student should be added to their personal list to master. The sight words that need reteaching should be placed in groups such as would, should, and could, or though, thought and through. Then prior to school and during the school year, five to ten words on their need-to-learn lists should be worked on each week until mastery occurs.

The weekly sight word learning lessons need not be dull or monotonous. Third and fourth graders can learn their five to ten words using colored washable markers, online games are available for free, and using plastic letters to make up spelling games. Adding fun to learning spelling words can create interest and improve mastery.

One fun way to help third and fourth graders learn to spell the sight words is to make spelling worksheets with the consonants written in but the vowels omitted. Then the child fills in the missing vowels from memory. Children enjoy playing hang-man-type games with their spelling words to add more fun to their learning sessions. Also, numerous children like to make up spelling cheers and raps to help them learn their lists. The spelling cheers or raps help add action to learning, which can assist the brain in mastering the words.

Children typically enjoy learning their spelling words by employing a game with a ball. The game can be played with one or more players. One player throws a ball to another participant, and the one who catches the ball must draw from a pile of words. The player with the ball then calls out the word for the person who threw the ball to spell. If the speller is able to spell the word correctly, they earn a point. If the word is misspelled, the player has to spell the words out loud three times before throwing it to the next player. This spelling game is a fun way for young students to learn their weekly spelling words with their family or peers.

Children also enjoy painting their spelling words on paper instead of writing them in pencil. Also, students may enjoy illustrating their list of words with washable paint. Others like to cut letters out of newspapers or magazines to use for spelling. Then they can spell the words with the cutout letters and glue them to a colored paper. They also typically enjoy writing their wording in large print or script in crayon and making designs around the words.

Third and fourth-grade students generally enjoy working on learning spelling lists when fun games and projects become part of the instructional processes. When students are having fun learning, they balk less and try hard to master new words. In addition, students can learn to enjoy the process of learning to spell words.

★ Prepare For Math Success

The days or weeks prior to the beginning of the new school year, third and fourth-grade students benefit from reviewing the basic math facts for approximately fifteen minutes daily. Refreshing and sharping students' recall and speed of access for the basic math facts can transform their mathematical skills. Centering the soon-to-be third or fourth-grade students' math review time around, improving their mastery of the basic math facts can also significantly reduce their time completing their math homework and daily assignments.

Third and fourth-grade students should spend the majority of their math review time completing paper-pencil math fact quiz sheets. The reason is to help assist the transference from their mind to paper. A reminder- the math fact quiz sheets can be found online or at a teacher supply store.

Third and fourth graders may need to have their math fact practice time split up into seven and a half minute sessions. They should first begin with the addition and subtraction facts and then move to the multiplication and division facts. Numerous third-grade students haven't learned the multiplication or division facts yet. Others have only learned a few of them. Therefore, they should practice the easier ones to master, such as the zeros. Ones, twos, threes, fives, and tens. Later, add in the fours and sixes. Pre-teaching can significantly assist students' ability to master the multiplication and division facts during the upcoming school year.

Third and fourth graders may balk at spending time reviewing the math facts. When students resist learning the math facts, gently remind them that this will save them time during the school year. It will also help them have an easier time learning new math procedures and score higher grades in their class. In my experience, students who have mastered and can quickly access the basic facts generally are better math students.

After a student completes one math fact sheet, then they should go over and correct the ones they missed. The facts the third or fourth graders missed should be presented on flashcards and reviewed for several minutes daily until mastery occurs. To add interest and motivation to learn the basic math facts allow the student to earn small rewards or no chores days. Adding a direct payoff or reward to the task can significantly inspire students to want to learn the facts and increase their diligence. Students may also want to take a short break between math fact sheets to move around and do some jumping jacks to help them focus when they start again.

When the school year begins, third and fourth graders benefit from continuing to work on learning the basic math facts for five to ten minutes daily. Over time the children will generally determine there is significant value in learning the basic math facts. They can also see an increase in the speed and accuracy of their ability to complete their math assignments. Students can learn to be fabulous math students.

★ Because You Asked

> *My daughter says she doesn't need to begin her homework and study schedule until after the first few weeks of school. She is going into third grade and feels her teacher won't be teaching very much anyway. What insight do you have about my daughter's request not to study during the first weeks of school?*

Thank you for your pertinent question. Your daughter, like many children, feels the initial weeks of school should be dedicated to getting adjusted. However, third graders greatly benefit from starting their study and homework routine on the first day of school. The rationale for this is even if your daughter doesn't have any assigned homework on the first days of school, she can use the time to get ahead start.

Third and fourth graders who start their homework and study routine on the first day of school benefit from their effort by putting themselves in a more academically successful place among their peers. Even if your child doesn't have assigned homework, the time can be spent pre-reading the first chapters of the textbooks or online sources, reading for improvement, practicing spelling words or personal lists, and reviewing math facts and procedures.

The time your daughter spending implementing her homework and study routine from the initial day of school can help her become a more academically organized and successful student. Even if your daughter balks, she may benefit from learning that getting ahead start can help her by making her more ready for her teacher's initial lessons in her classroom.

★ Mom's Space By Karen Dianis

A new school year brings hope and expectations of educational success to parents and their students. However, more than half of the student population will experience academic glitches during the new school year. Children who begin the school year with a head start normally will perform better than they would if they are always playing the try-to-catch-up game.

Therefore, starting the school year off from the initial day of the school week, implementing a homework and study routine can help prevent academic difficulties. It can also help students with educational problems in one or more core subject areas overcome them at a faster rate. The beginning of a new school year is an exciting time for children. Parents who capitalize on beginning the school year off strong can help transform their children's grades throughout their educational journey. Happy August and the new school year to all!

September

Learning Strategies To Help Children Begin The School Year Academically Strong

September

The crisp autumn air waft through the streets, reminding children that the first whole month of school has arrived. The sights of the school buses are everywhere as the loud roar of their engines is heard for miles. Students had almost forgotten the presence of the yellow school buses during the past months. However, now they have filled the roadways once again. Parents are further reminded of the new school year as crosswalks, crossing guards, and flashing school zone signs have reappeared.

At the beginning of a new school year, children are typically eager to return to a routine and make more friends. In the initial weeks of school, third and fourth graders are generally more optimistic about school. However, students who have struggled academically in the past years and have developed negative feelings toward school generally can learn how to experience educational success for the first time. Struggling students can learn how to become proactive towards their subjects instead of reactive.

Staring the school year off strong is possible even if third or fourth graders have experienced academic difficulties in the past. The feeling of academic success can help propel struggling students toward new study and organizational habits. Struggling students can learn to succeed academically!

★ Daily Brag Time To Improve Children's Attitude Toward School

Students from all grade levels can find themselves becoming less favorable toward school and learning. Even from the initial days of school, students may find they are experiencing negative feelings regarding one or more subject areas. Therefore, a daily brag time has assisted numerous students in adapting a more cheerful toward school.

At the end of each school day or in the evening, students benefit from discussing what they did well in their school day with their families. Students want to feel they did well in school even if they are struggling academically. Providing a platform to express positive aspects of the school day can help students restore their positive attitude toward learning. The *Daily Brag Time* can help children find the good in their day. Focusing on the fun aspects of school can be helpful to improve their feeling toward learning and attending school.

Students benefit from positive feedback for what they did well in school, especially if they are experiencing academic struggles. Children benefit from feeling that they have done some praiseworthy deeds each day. Daily bragging about how they did well can help students learn to transform their thoughts from negative toward positive ones throughout their lives.

Children who learn how to transform their negative feelings toward school into positive ones often find their attitude can affect their educational achievement. The *Daily Brag Time* can dramatically prevent children from drifting into students with lowered academic self-esteem. In addition, this technique can help ease children's feeling of educational anxiety and help them become more confident students.

★ How Do Parents Know When To Respond To Academic Struggles?

At the initial month or months of a new school year, children's academic struggles are easily seen as ones that will dissipate. Therefore, once deemed only as scholastic glitches or issues go un-remediated. In my professional opinion, it is better to respond to an educational slide as soon as it begins to occur. The reason is learning builds upon itself. Generally, when high school students experience difficulty in one or more subjects, their learning deficiencies can be traced to unlearned or unmastered concepts from their elementary years.

Unmastered core learning concepts can be the catalyst to further academic issues as students progress in their educational journey. In addition, third or fourth graders may continue to slide academically and may lack the ability to remediate themselves. Therefore, as soon as an academic issue becomes apparent, it should be re-mediated at home to help prevent further scholastic struggles. Parents who are proactive towards their children's learning slides often find their students regaining their academic edge.

★ How Do Parents Know When Academic Issues Are Hindering Their Child's Learning?

Third and fourth-grade students may tend not to verbalize their academic difficulties or hide their lower graded papers and tests. Subsequently, parents may find themselves not fully realizing their child is sliding in one or more academic areas until they receive their child's first report card.

September

    In today's modern technological world, most teachers must post their students' grades on private online web pages. Parents should check their child's grades online several times per week. It is also beneficial to go through their child's graded assignments, which should be filed in folders or a notebook. As the parent peruses their child's classwork and test grades, they should look for areas where their child is scoring low or low average grades. The area in which their child appears not to be mastering should be re-mediated and retaught during study time.

    Parents will find their child will benefit from incorporating reteaching and re-remedial learning over unmastered concepts. The reteaching can come from going over what their child missed and reteaching the idea. It should also consist of the child correcting their mistakes on their daily work or tests. Some students will need further work on concepts in order for mastery to occur. Additional instructional information can be found online, or ask their teacher for more assignments covering the same concepts. In addition, more learning assignments can be found at the back of their learning text, teacher supply store, or online classroom source. Parents can also make up some learning material that reteaches specific concepts. The techniques which will be presented throughout this book can make a difference in learning being mastered. The concepts should be gone over for several weeks until true mastery has occurred. A sign of mastery is their child has transferred the idea from their short-term memory to their long-term memory.

★ Reading Improvement Strategies For Success

Reading problems in third and fourth-grade students, which go un-remediated, can cause students to fall behind in their studies throughout their educational journey. According to the *Barbara Bush Foundation for Reading*, 85% of students who finished their fourth-grade year behind in their reading skills will never catch up, and most become high school dropouts. That is a staggering statistic, which was represented as accurately as of 2021. Subsequently, one can conclude that it is imperative that third and fourth graders work hard to increase and improve their reading skills consistently. That generally means students need to work on progressing in their reading skills up and beyond what is being taught or expected in their classroom curriculums.

Initially, third and fourth graders benefit from being pre-taught the words they are unfamiliar with before they are introduced in their classroom. Parents should go through the story in their children's reading textbook the evening before it will be taught in class. Students and their parents can make a list of new words, which will be introduced in the story.

The new word list can be written in two colors using colored pencils. The consonants should be written in one color. The vowel or phonetic spellings such as *igh or ite* can be written in another color. The use of two different colors assists students' ability to use the phonetic rules to decode and blend words that are new to them. The latest word lists should be gone over at least five to ten times to help provide children with more instances to learn them.

Next, third and fourth-grade students benefit from pre-reading the new reading story before it is taught in their class. The student and their parent or older sibling should help them point out the words they encounter from their new word list. If the student misreads the new word, then it should be re-read five to ten times by the child. This strategy will help children master new words at a faster rate. As the child re-reads the new word, the phonetic rule(s) it follows should be said several times to help students master the phonetic rules.

Then in the morning, the new story will be presented in their classroom; the student and their parent should go over the new word list once or twice. The continued repetition helps children retain the words. If specific words are challenging for the student to master, the words should be added to a running reading list and the words reviewed daily until mastery occurs. Again, the words added to the student's personal running reading list should be written by the student in two different colors to demonstrate the phonetic rule(s) found in the word.

Students should have a running reading list of words to master throughout the school year, even if they are reading at grade level or above. The running reading word list can be changed as the student masters the words on the list. There should be a list of words to be quickly reviewed from time to time in order to prevent the student from forgetting the reading words they have previously learned.

Consistent repetition is one of the keys to help children with learning issues or glitches to become better readers. In addition, many children with Dyslexia may need to trace the letters of the words using a small chalkboard and chalk.

Tracing over the letters with chalk or their fingers can help bring more tactile feedback and help the brain retain the information better.

Third and fourth-grade students also benefit from having their running reading list posted in several places in their homes. The running reading list should be posted in areas that the child frequents. The running reading list for independent practice should include the phonetic pronunciation of the word. This technique will help students be able to decode the words easier and aid in retention. Students with reading challenges can become excellent readers even if they have Dyslexia. The consistent application of proven reading strategies has helped numerous students learn how to catch up in their reading. These proven strategies have also helped countless students become above-average readers for their consistent efforts toward remediation. Third and fourth grades can learn to become excellent readers!

★ Reading Comprehension Tips

Third and fourth graders have now moved into the grade levels where they are now learning to read and reading to learn. Most all subject areas, even math, are impacted by students' ability to comprehend what they read. Therefore, the ability to understand and retain what one is reading is perhaps the most essential academic skill. Sadly, when students struggle with their reading comprehension skills, they often experience academic difficulties throughout their academic years.

The good news is that third and fourth graders can learn how to improve their reading comprehension skills using their daily homework assignments. Young students benefit from perusing their assigned reading material before they begin reading. While they are looking over their assigned reading pages, they should be reading captions under the pictures, bold print words with their explanations, and chapter headings. This method will provide students with an overview of the assigned reading and what it's designed to teach. Then children should read each paragraph then stop and say aloud one to three ideas they just read. This strategy helps prevent students from just reading the words and forgetting to focus on their reading.

Next, after the child has read the entire assignment one time, they should re-read it again to gain further information. Typically, students rush through the reading in order to be finished. Thence, they miss key details and forget what they have read. By requiring the child to read the text or assignment two to three times, each helps them retain more of the information to be learned. In addition, the multiple read-throughs will provide students with reading decoding, blending, and fluency practice.

★ Homework And Study Time Organizational Tips

Students of all ages waste valuable time going on endless searches for homework and study supplies. Some even appear to be on an archeological dig when looking for their items. Therefore, to help save numerous hours, a study and homework supply crate or box can be a lifesaver. As soon as your student's school supplies are purchased, please place them in a study crate or box that will be used throughout the year to store their school supplies.

Students should place all of their supplies back into their crate or box at the end of each homework and study session. The school crate or container should be stored in the same area so that it won't need to be found as well. This technique can save countless hours and eliminate needless frustration for parents and their students.

Next, students should be provided with a place to do their homework and study that is not in their room. This strategy is because students may become highly distracted by other objects, toys, phones, etcetera. When the additional temptations beaconing students to more fun activities can greatly slow down their learning time. It is generally better for students to complete their homework and study where other family members can see them. The third and fourth-grade students can be monitored to make sure they are working on their assignments. In addition, they can easily ask for assistance or have their work spot checked for accuracy. Providing students with a set study place and homework crate or box can be a fabulous time saver.

★ Because You Asked

> *Homework is my child's total responsibility, which is what my son's teachers have told me. I have also been encouraged not to help with homework. If I do provide homework assistance, it should only be sparely given. What advice can*

September

you give me about how often and how much homework help I should give my son when he struggles in several academic subjects.

Thank you for your pertinent question. It is my professional opinion that when a student is struggling or performing at average or below average in one or more subject areas, help should be provided. When one examines the purpose of homework, they discover it is to give students additional practice on essential grade-level skills. The assignments are also to help students learn new skills and master core curriculum material.

Therefore, if a child is not accurately completing their assignments in one or more subject area(s), the purpose of homework is not being met. It doesn't seem that when students complete assignments incorrectly is very productive in regards to teaching skills. Moreover, the additional reinforcement of learning a skill poorly typically does more academic damage than good.

Using coaches' techniques as an example can help parents achieve a more accurate picture to apply to the homework issue. If a coach allowed a student on a team to practice skills incorrectly continually, everyone would be outraged at the coach. The student-athlete would have non-useable sports skills. Consequently, if a student is not completing their homework or assignments accurately, then additional assistance and re-teaching should be provided to the child. If and when this happens, then go back over the directions and key concepts with your child. Next, help your student with several of the problems or questions until they are able to apply the concept independently. If your student struggles to learn the skill, keep re-teaching it using more information from their school text, an online source, or study books. Over time your child will benefit from the additional instruction and reach mastery at a faster rate. Homework time is to reinforce and reteach core concepts learning skills.

★ Dad's Space By David Dianis

As a caring Dad, I felt it was part of my responsibility to help my children apply math skills in their daily lives. When I took my children to the store, I would have them pay the bill with money. Then I would ask my children to calculate the change I should receive on my purchases after they knew the amount. I asked the cashier not to tell them the amount of change. I would give each of my children a few coins if they correctly calculated to change to be given back to me. The incentive to receive a few coins added extra motivation for them to come up with the correct number.

If the cashier were very busy, I would have him, or her just give me my change without verbalizing it and have my children turn around so they wouldn't be able to read the cash register. If one or both of my children answered incorrectly, I would go over the answer and calculate it with them. This fun math technique helped my children improve their math skills while having some fun with their Dad. Happy September to all!

October

Learning Ideas And Proven Strategies For Grade Improvement

October

The cooler crisp air and shorter daylight hours are announcing fall is now in its first full calendar month. The brilliant, vibrant leaves are bursting into their majestic colors. Fall sports are ending soon, and young teams are trying to make the playoffs. Now that fall is here; the third and fourth grades begin to dream of the arrival of the holiday season.

The past days of summer seem to children like years away, as the new school year now comes to the point that a more challenging curriculum is being introduced. The pace, volume, and complexity of the third and fourth-grade curriculums are steadily increasing. Children may often find their homework load is becoming larger as the calendar turns from one month into another.

Some third and fourth graders have already received their first report card if they are on a six-week system. Regardless of the grading schedule, new report cards will soon be given to students and their parents. The early report cards can highlight academic problems that will need to be remediated or show potential learning issues that can possibly be avoided with some techniques. They can also illuminate academic strengths, which should be celebrated.

As the school year continues, third and fourth graders struggling in one or more academic areas should increase their study time by 5 to 7 minutes a day. The extra time devoted to studying will help third and fourth grades improve in their areas of difficulties and help them work toward overcoming them.

★ Fall Parent Teach Conference Tips

Fall parent-teacher conferences are an essential part of children's educational journey. According to the *Graham Study of 2006, students are more likely to drop out of school if they don't have a parent who participates with their school teachers or communicates with the school.* Therefore, it can be concluded that parents who attend parent-teacher conferences are helping their children work toward the goal of high school graduation. Some parents may feel they can skip the fall conference, but that can lead to school problems in the future for their son or daughter.

Numerous parents often walk into parent-teacher conferences without being prepared and often can become overwhelmed with the tone and implications of what the teacher is conveying regarding their child. As an Educational Specialist with years of experience, it is my professional opinion that parents can help solve and prevent scholastic issues by being prepared for the conference.

Grade Transformer for the Modern Student

First, parents can significantly benefit from keeping an educational portfolio of their children's graded papers. The parents may wish to file their child's graded papers and tests in an accordion-style folder with each division for a different subject. The reason for the graded papers portfolio is that the papers will provide the teacher and parent with a complete picture of the actual skill level of the student. When an academic problem is mentioned, the graded papers and tests can provide detailed information on the fundamental academic glitch. They can also provide the parent and teacher with a snapshot of academic areas that are going well for the student.

The additional information the graded papers portfolio provides can significantly assist the parent and teacher in finding ways to remediate the student's areas of school weaknesses. During the conference time, a plan of action should be discussed regarding how to help the child back on the road to academic success.

The portfolio can also represent that the parent values their child's education and is willing to participate in the solution. In addition, at times, teachers will become so focused on discussing academic problems that they end up skewing the conference to make the problem(s) seem worse than they really are. The teacher may also show papers representing the school issues only and not discuss the areas of strengths and the graded papers completed at an average or above-average level.

Next, the parent should bring their own list of questions for the teacher regarding their child's academics. The list of questions should include one or two questions asking the teacher what they will do to assist their student in their areas of educational struggles. When there are academic areas of concern, it takes extra effort from the teacher, student, and parents to close the student's learning gaps.

Then parents need to take notes over what the teacher says in order to refer back to them to help their students remediate the learning challenges. The notes should be stored in a place where they will be easily accessible for this year and future years. The reason for this is if your child has difficulty in the later grade levels, you will have your notes to help you detect trends for remediation. Also, the fall conference notes can serve as a guide to make sure consistent remediation is taking place. Lastly, the notes can help you determine if measurable improvement has happened after several months.

October

★ Discussing Academic Issues After The Fall Conference With Your Child Tips

Numerous parents are uncertain what information from the fall conferences to discuss with their child if there are academic issues. Third and fourth-grade students generally internally know when they are not keeping pace with their classmates in one or more subject areas. When parents have a chance to go over the conference notes and have had time to process the information, it can help present it to their child. First, begin with some compliments of what they are doing correctly or excelling in. Even if they seem to be really struggling in school, there will be some items that can be complemented, such as effort, attitude, and diligence.

Next, go over the area or areas of concern. Then let your child know you are on their side and in their corner. Go over ways that you can help them strengthen their academic weaknesses. Lastly, discuss the idea that there will be areas of struggle that present themselves in most peoples' lives, and learning how to work through problems early in life can bring rewards later on. Then work on adding ten-twenty extra minutes daily to their study routine to address their educational issues specifically. This book will provide the student and parent with proven educational strategies that can help to transform their academic abilities.

★ Reward The Small Victories To Help Lead To Bigger Ones

The remediation process can take some time to complete if the student is six or more months academically behind their peers. The child typically will have some scholastic victories on their way toward remediation. The small victories should be celebrated because students need consistent positive reinforcement. Every time a child scores several points higher than the last, they benefit from receiving tokens or tickets toward a reward.

The rewards for scholastic improvement don't have to be money-based. They can be redeemed for a no-chore night, weekend, or week. They can be for a family game night or movie night. The key is to find what motivates your child and what rewards they will be more willing to work toward earning.

In my years as an Educational Specialist, I found that most students with learning issues are seldom rewarded for their academic efforts. Therefore, the at-home reward system for even small educational victories can serve to level the playing field for a struggling student. When the small victories are appreciated, then typically, larger ones will follow over time. The additional positive reinforcement can help struggling students gain a better attitude toward school and serve as motivators. Remember, most everyone enjoys being rewarded for their efforts and hard work.

★ Math Improvement Now Tips

Math classrooms are filled with students of all ages and walks of life who can't understand why they are so completely confused during the classroom instructional lessons. Millions of students across the globe sit in math lectures, unable to make sense of the teacher's instructions. Many will find their minds wandering off and maybe looking out a window instead of being focused on the day's teaching.

Over the years, the above scenario presented itself often enough to inspire investigation into why so many students find math so difficult to understand. After years of talking to math-challenged students and working to help them overcome their math problems, I found that so many students didn't know the vocabulary of math. Even when I was a middle school math teacher, I discovered that the students who were struggling didn't have a clear understanding of the terminology associated with math. Therefore, one of the initial ways to help a math-challenged student is to teach them the vocabulary of math.

First, look through your third or fourth grader's math textbook or online source. Look at the vocabulary words they will need to understand and make a list of the mathematical terms. Then ask your son or daughter what each of the words means in relation to math. If they are unable to answer correctly, make a check by the word to be learned. Many parents will find they will need to go back through several chapters and check their child's knowledge of mathematical vocabulary terms.

Third and fourth grades benefit from being reminded that math concepts build upon themselves, and they will need to have the terms mastered for this year and the upper grades. Then make fun flashcards with your child with the math word on one side and the definition on the other. Numerous students benefit from drawing an illustration of the math term to go along with the definition. The illustration of the math term can serve as a visual reminder of what the word truly means in relation to math.

Next, go over five to ten math terms daily until mastery occurs and then add more mathematical vocabulary words to their pile of words to be learned. Third and fourth graders will soon find they are generally able to understand and comprehend more of their math teacher's lessons. In addition, they will also find they may be more focused during their classroom instruction because the lessons are making more sense to the student.

In addition, third and fourth graders can significantly benefit from being taught the mathematical terms they will be learning in class in the upcoming week during the weekend. Students often determine that being introduced to the math vocabulary and developing a foundational knowledge of the words helps them perform better in class. This method can, in turn, help students develop higher levels of confidence because they are increasing their mathematical understanding of the classroom lessons. The additional time third and fourth graders dedicate to learning the vocabulary of math can have great rewards in understanding and faster mastery of concepts. They often feel they are no longer left feeling defeated and confused every time their teacher begins a new mathematical lesson. In turn, they generally feel more confident and eager to learn new arithmetic concepts.

★ Spelling Grade Improvement Quick Tip

Third and fourth-grade students convey that they studied all week for their classroom weekly spelling test only to be handed their test paper with a low score recorded at the top. They generally feel disappointed, and some may feel as if their efforts to master the spelling list are in vain. Others find themselves remembering the correct spelling of some of the words later in the day, such as when they are at lunch or on the playground.

Subsequently, since this is an all too common spelling glitch the solution, I helped my students implement worked wonders to improve their spelling scores. On Friday morning, which is typically the day of the spelling test, ask your son or daughter to go over the spelling words with you prior to them leaving for school. They should also briefly review their spelling list while on the way to school in order to help them retain the words. The time young students spend reviewing the morning of the test can significantly help them improve their grades in spelling. It can also motivate them to continue to put forth effort each week to learning their classroom spelling lists.

★ Because You Asked

After school, almost always, my son complains about having to do his homework and carries on for nearly an hour before he reluctantly starts working on his assignments. How can I help him understand his complaining is not helping him?

Thank you for your pertinent question. It appears as if your son hasn't realized that the time he spends venting about his homework is essentially hindering his free time. By your description, it seems as if your son may benefit from having a break before he sits down to complete his assignments. Numerous students of all ages need time for themselves after school before returning to working on scholastics again.

Remember, your son has already spent the majority of his day working on academics and may need some time for other activities before beginning his homework. Try to work out a system that transfers his complaining time into free time. Then after he has enjoyed a break from work, he may be more ready to work on his assignments.

Children generally respond well to feeling like they are part of the decision-making of when homework is to be done each school day. The break time can help him refresh and be ready to settle down to complete his assignments. In addition, for each week he doesn't complain about his homework, you may want to reward his positive attitude with something like choosing a game to play with your family.

Third and fourth graders typically feel more positive and encouraged when they are working toward a reward for transforming their negative attitudes. This technique can also help him to feel more listened to and understood. The change of schedule can help him be able to see that his needs are also being taken into consideration. Homework and study time don't need to be a daily conflict and can become a more optimistic time of the school day. Homework can become a happy and productive time for children!

October

★ Mom's Space By Karen Dianis

October is a fabulous month to help usher in the holiday months by completing some themed-centered learning activities during the weekends. The themes can be football or holiday reading and reading comprehension stories. Third and fourth grades can benefit from reading fun fall grade level and age-appropriate stories and answering comprehension questions regarding what they just read. The comprehension questions can be made by a parent or from a reading comprehension workbook. The seasonally-themed reading comprehension workbooks can be found online or at teacher's supply stores.

An elementary-age student generally enjoys the seasonal reading comprehension stories. They can improve their listening, focusing, and retention skills by answering story-based questions. Students can go over any missed answer question with a parent or older sibling. The student should be encouraged to go back over the story and locate the correct answer. This educational technique can help inspire students to learn to enjoy reading during the weekends. Happy October to all!

November

Learning Strategies To Help Children Improve Their Grades

November

The crisper late fall days that will rapidly transform into the holiday season have arrived. Fall sports and activities are soon to be replaced with winter ones. The hours of daylight have now shortened. The air is becoming chillier, signaling the ending of fall is not far away. In November, third and fourth graders' minds will begin to wander toward the upcoming holidays.

Meanwhile, the school year is well on its way as the year is heading toward the halfway point. School routines have been well established as the school year continues to become more complex. The rate, volume, and complexity of the curriculum are now accelerating at a steady pace.

Currently, third and fourth graders are now learning scholastic concepts that will become the foundation of numerous amount of educational high school concepts. Young students are often unaware that the core learning objectives and the material will serve as a basis for their future academic studies. Surprisingly, many subject area glitches upper-grade students experience can be found to be rooted in unmastered or forgotten lower grade concepts. Therefore, third and fourth-grade students need to understand that the educational knowledge they are learning now will help them achieve better grades in their future classes. This idea can help motivate third and fourth-grade students to become diligent academic workers. The strategy can also help students understand the remediation of unmastered skills is very important.

November is the month to add 5 to 10 minutes a day of additional study and review time to every class they are not performing at a high average or better level. The added remedial time can produce dramatically better grades as a result. The academic turnaround may take several weeks or more to show up in their grades, but their efforts will generally pay off in the overtime. As the curriculum begins to reach the holiday season, parents should pay close attention to their student's grades online to ensure all of their students' assignments are being turned in. This strategy will also help parents to be aware of tests and announced quizzes that will need to be prepared for to ensure higher grades. With all of its fun and activities, the holiday season can leave students with lower grades and missing assignments.

Subsequently, careful homework and study time planning are essential to ensure that third and fourth-grade students' grades continue on an upward path. In addition, parents and their students benefit from using a calendar to fill in all of the special holiday activities, parties, and long-term assignments.

Then they should plan their homework and study times around the different holiday events to help them finish the initial part of the school year off strong. This technique will help the third and fourth grades learn valuable executive management skills. Third and fourth grades can finish the first half of the school year strong while enjoying the holiday festivities.

★ Long Term Assignments And Report Strategies To Help Children Earn Higher Grades And Improve Their Organizational Skills

As the latter half of the first semester of school arrives, children typically will be assigned one or more long-term assignments and reports. Students of all ages find it tempting to procrastinate over their project or report start date. All too often, students wait until a night or two prior to the due date to begin working on their long-term assignment or report. Subsequently, the typical student meltdown and marathon begin. Frustrated parents then try to help their child complete an assignment intended to be done over several weeks.

The day the long-term assignment is given out in class, students should work with their parents on designing a plan to complete it in small sections. The large assignment instructions should be read over three times before it is broken down into manageable parts. Next, all of the steps should be highlighted in one color. The steps should be numbered in a bold color to help ensure students realize the number of steps to be completed. This technique also assists children in self-checking each step to make sure they have been done and not skipped.

Next, children with their parents should determine how much of the long-term project should be completed each evening. It is usually good for the student to have the long-term project completed a week prior to the due date. The reason for this is to provide the students time to make any revisions or tweak their project to improve it. Finishing long-term projects early help instill good organizational skills that will be useful in their future grade levels.

After the third or fourth grader has set out a step-by-step procedure for completion, they should begin the brainstorming process. Brainstorming and thinking through the project is an excellent way to help children use their creativity to create an impressive long-term project or report. The brainstorming can be done on paper, and the child can draw their ideas if they prefer. Then the ideas should be narrowed down to the ones that will make their project or report more impressive.

Next, a list of supplies and learning resources should be made and include information on where to locate them. Then students benefit from filling out a to be done list every evening on a calendar to help keep them on track. The long-term assignment or report should be worked on for approximately twenty minutes each school day. The limited-time typically helps young students remain excited about their assignments and focused on their work.

Each day that the young child completes the portion of their long-term assignment, they should receive a tally mark that will count toward a reward. The incentive they work for can be a family game night or ones not necessarily monetary related. The addition of a reward for staying on a schedule helps end conflicts and possible meltdowns.

Prior to beginning the long-term project or report each evening, the child should reread the instructions to help him or her to improve their direction reading and understanding skills. Then each step is carefully completed each evening. Next, the child and a parent should go over the work in order to check for accuracy. Through the completion process, each step should be checked off the list of ones to be done. Every step should also be evaluated to see if further corrections are necessary. This strategy helps improve organizational and following directions skills.

Students who learn to design and stick to a step-by-step schedule when long-term assignments are given out generally score higher grades for their efforts. They learn valuable organizational skills. This method also helps students from giving in to the temptation to procrastinate and put off the work until the eleventh hour.

★ Find Impressive Sources For Long-Term Projects And Reports

When third and fourth graders are assigned long-term assignments and reports, they will need to back up their claims with good sources. However, numerous third and fourth-grade students are often uncertain of where to locate quality sources. One good place to begin locating sources is in their school library. Most school libraries have numerous research books that can be used as excellent sources. The local public library is another wonderful place to find sources.

Students benefit from locating resource information from sources that are not always only ones from the Internet. Third and fourth grades should look for additional sources online that fulfill their teacher's requirements for quality sources. Third and fourth graders typically benefit from being reminded that not all Internet resource information will be accepted as quality and accurate sources. Before your student begins their research, please check their list of references to help them determine if their teacher will accept them.

In numerous instances, young students may begin their research and use sources which their teacher won't allow. This method can result in a significant loss of points deducted from their work. If a third or fourth grader is unsure about one or more of their research sources, they should ask their teacher. Once their sources are located and approved by their teacher, they should begin their long-term assignment. It is commonly better for students to gather their project or report sources within the first three days of the assignment being given by their teacher. The earlier the third and fourth grades learn to begin working on their long-term work, the better their future organizational skills will often be. Young students can learn how to find quality sources to help them earn higher grades on their long-term assignments.

★ Written Language Improvement Tips

The academic area of written language is one of the most important and complex of all learning skills. Subsequently, countless students demonstrate difficulties writing their thoughts on paper. However, third and fourth-grade students can learn how to demonstrate above-average and impressive writing skills.

When faced with writing assignments, numerous students will convey they can't think of anything to write about that interests them. Others will look over the suggested topics from their teacher and feel they cannot come up with ideas to write about on the list. Numerous students will sit for long periods of time staring at their paper with very little work accomplished. Some third and fourth graders will begin writing on a topic and lose their focus. Countless students begin on topic. However, as they continue writing, they become off-topic in their writing. Some students will add sentences that don't fit with their selected subject and do not realize they have added irreverent details. The good news is there are techniques that can help students improve their written language skills.

First, the student should thoroughly read the instructions several times. Then the child benefits from numbering each step that is to be completed. Next, the student should highlight each step needed to fulfill the requirement of the writing assignment. Once the third or fourth grader has broken down the instructions into steps and found quality sources to back up their claims, they are ready to begin their assignment.

Students benefit from brainstorming ideas they have gathered from the quality sources they are using for their assignment. Third and fourth graders should begin with the brainstorming lists they have already constructed and determined which ideas will be the strongest to prove their points. Then the issues to use in their written language paper should be numbered in sequence to be included in the written language assignments.

Next, the student should narrow down their topic ideas to write about by including two or three per paragraph. Some teachers will want their students to include four per paragraph. Students generally benefit from pre-writing the middle sentences in their six to nine-sentence paragraphs.

However, when students believe they don't know how to write their sentences on paper, they should verbally say what they think about the topic. When students say what they are thinking instead of writing the sentence, they generally construct a more interesting sentence. *Write what you just said* is an excellent way to help students improve their written language skills. If your third or fourth grader has some difficulty writing down what they said, then a parent may wish to help them record their thoughts. Then the child can refer back to their recorded thoughts to include the most pertinent ones in their assignment.

Next, encourage your third or fourth graders to write the factual sentences first. Then they should write one or more describing sentences for each factual sentence. Most teachers will specify how many sentences they want to be included in each paragraph. Students should be reminded that nine sentences are generally the largest amount to use per paragraph. Most third and fourth graders should strive to write eight-sentence paragraphs unless their teacher's directions require a different number of sentences per paragraph. After the six factual and descriptions, sentences have been written, and each one should be examined for clarity, impressive adverbs, quality adjectives, and proper punctuation.

Third and fourth graders benefit from looking through their sentences and replacing two common words per sentence with more impressive ones with the same or very similar meanings. Students can use a thesaurus to look up common words and change them to impressive synonyms. Exchanging common words into higher-level synonyms helps create excellent writing skills that young students will use in the higher grades.

Next, third and fourth graders should check each of their sentences for capitalization and ending punctuation marks. Numerous students concentrate so hard on writing their paragraphs that they forget to use proper punctuation. Therefore, students who learn to self-check their work for punctuation will find they will score higher grades throughout their academic years. Then students benefit from re-reading each of their sentences for clarity. Parents or an older sibling may help students determine if a word is missing or if the sentences make sense and flow together with the others in the paragraph.

After checking the middle sentences of the paragraph then the introduction sentence is written. The reason for writing the introduction sentences after the middle sentences is to help students stay on topic. Countless students write great topic sentences that don't follow their middle sentences and are downgraded as a result. Lastly, the concluding sentence is written. The conclusion sentence generally restates the introduction one with different wording and may include a finding from the middle sentences.

Students benefit from re-reading each of their paragraphs aloud to family or friends to ensure they aren't missing information or wording. Costly mistakes can be caught and corrected before their work is turned in for grading. Then they benefit from reviewing the written directions to make sure they are continuing to follow them. Next, third and fourth graders benefit from repeating the same steps for the remainder of their assignment. When they are finished, they should recheck the written directions to ensure each step has been completed correctly. Over time third and fourth graders' written language skills can significantly improve by utilizing the above strategies.

★ Grammar Skills Improvement Quick Fixes

As the third and fourth grades continue in their education, they will be learning how to apply correct grammar skills to their daily written work. Unfortunately, some school curriculums have cut back on teaching grammar in all grade levels. Regardless if the students are learning grammar rules or not, they still need to master them. One fun way to help third and fourth graders learn the parts of speech is to make collages to illustrate them.

Students typically enjoy making grammar skills collages to help them master the parts of speech. First, the students should take a large piece of construction paper and divide it into three sections the long way. Then label each section with one of the parts of speech, such as verbs, adjectives, and adverbs. Under the part of speech, the students benefit from writing the definition of the part of speech.

Next, students can use old magazines, newspapers, cartoons, clip art from the Internet, old coloring books to represent visual images of each part of speech. The pictures can also be drawn. Each picture is to be glued under the corresponding column for the part of speech and definition. Then the collage can help provide students with concrete examples of the parts of speech. When one collage is finished, the students can then make other ones to represent nouns, prepositions, conjunctions, interjections, and pronouns. Students may benefit from placing cut-out words or labeling the pictures to help increase understanding. Conjunctions may be represented in the collage by using words or print cut-out words.

The parts of speech collages can assist third and fourth graders in mastering the eight parts of speech. They can serve as visual reminders of each of the grammar terms, which the student can see every day.

The collages can be made during the holiday breaks if students feel they don't have the time until a break to make them. Parts of speech collage-making can be a fun way to entertain children during school holiday breaks. Fun learning crafts can help teach students valuable grammar while having a good time learning. Holiday breaks can be a wonderful time for students to learn while having fun.

★ Because You Asked

> *According to her reading assessment skill testing, my fourth grader is more than a year behind in her reading. Now that the holiday breaks are coming up, she says she wants to take a complete break from her studies. Since she is reading below her grade level, should she spend some time during the holidays to work on bringing up her reading skills?*

Thank you for your question. Numerous students feel they want to take a total break from their studies during the holiday breaks. However, if your child is reading below their grade level, the holidays can be a terrific time for students to work on bringing up their scholastic skills.

Ask your daughter to spend an hour and a half per day on school vacation to improve her reading skills. The first half an hour should be spent on learning new reading words by making word lists that follow specific phonics rules. The phonics rules can be selected by taking an oral reading informal assessment of the word types she frequently misreads when reading aloud. Then make a list of the misread words and categorize them into like phonetic sounds.

Next, locate like words that follow the same phonetic rules. Like phonetic type words can be found in a dictionary or online source. The word lists should be presented one at a time. Next, help your daughter decode and read them orally as many times as needed until mastery eventually occurs.

The next half an hour can be spent on learning and working on mastering any sight words she cannot read. Again, an information reading inventory can be taken to assess her ability to read the *Dolch Sight Words*. A list of the sight words can be found online, at the public library, or her school should be able to provide you with a copy. Then the words can be introduced five to ten at a time. The words should be gone over each day until mastery occurs.

The final thirty minutes can be spent reading orally out of her school reader, an online source, or high-interest books that are a month or so over her reading level. When your daughter must decode a word, help her by going over the phonetic rules found in the word.

The reading improvement time can be divided into three-time increments if needed. After your daughter completes her reading remediation sessions each day, you may wish to provide her with redeemable points for family rewards. Most children are more motivated to work on their academics if they feel their work is being rewarded. Holiday breaks are an ideal time for students to work on improving their scholastic skills.

★ Mom's Space Fractions Tips By Karen Dianis

The upcoming holiday season is a wonderful time to bake with your third or fourth grader. Holiday baking can help teach children about fractions. Using measuring cups and spoons can help provide students with visual images of

November

how much common fractions are of a whole. Also, by doubling or tripling a recipe, students can learn how to add fractions. If a recipe is too large, then subtracting an amount such as a fourth, third, or half can help students learn how to subtract them. Holiday baking can be a fun way to help your children learn fractions while learning how to follow recipes. Happy November to everyone.

December

Learning Strategies For To
Help Elevate Grades

December

Everywhere one looks, the sights, sounds, and smells of the holidays fill third and fourth graders with anticipation of fun times that will be arriving soon. The shorter days and cooler temperatures have arrived. The fabulous holiday decorations are a reminder that soon, they will be taking a break from school. Third and fourth graders can hardly believe they will soon be finishing the first half of the school year. As the end of the first semester of the school year is near, students will need academic tips and strategies to help them finish strong.

The holiday season brings additional activities along with the end of the semester academic commitments. Therefore, the general populace of third and fourth grades can use additional organizational and educational strategies to finish the semester on an upward note. Young students who improve their grades prior to the end of the year will often find a renewed sense of scholastic self-esteem. They can also experience greater grade success in the new year and help make the second semester more positive.

Parents, during one of the busiest times of the year, it is very easy to wavier away from an academic homework and study schedule. Adults are also running more errands and have additional holiday activities along with their children's extra events. To help keep students' academics on track during this special time, I recommend several methods.

First, find a desktop calendar during the end of November or at the beginning of December. Next, fill it in with all of the dates and times of the special activities you already know about the times they will take place. Then as invitations and notices come in, add them to the family calendar. Next, peruse the calendar and find the necessary forty-five minutes to an hour each day for your child to do his or her homework and study for tests. The homework time may be different for each day of the week. The homework and study time may need to be divided into smaller segments in order to fit every activity you choose to do.

Children benefit from working on their homework on the way home from school and while riding in the car to activities. Sometimes third and fourth graders can complete half or more of their homework while transient from one place to another. Utilizing as much smaller time frames can help third and fourth graders stay on track during this busy and fun time. This technique can also lessen stress about not getting the work done. In addition, it can help prevent late-night homework and study sessions that were delayed because of evening activities. Students will also learn how to stay organized while participating in more events than what is typically normal for them.

The weekends of holiday months are great for students to catch up and complete some of their assignments ahead of time. Numerous classroom academic schedules are posted online, and parents can generally view the upcoming week's work by the Friday before. Using that information, students can get a head start on learning their class's spelling words, reading their assigned reading, and completing some other work they have in their workbooks or from their class online source. These tips can help third and fourth graders finish the school year scholastically strong while enjoying the additional holiday events and activities.

★ Test-Taking Tips To Help Children Earn Better Test Scores

The word test can send chills through the most confident of students and cause anxiety to numerous others. For generations, students have dreaded the word test. This apprehension may be based on students' negative experiences with the test-taking process. Third and fourth grades often don't realize that the ability to take tests and score higher grades can be taught to low test takers. Elementary students who want to apply strategies to help them can master the art of test-taking.

Proficient test-taking skills can assist students throughout their educational journey by helping them earn higher grades. Students can also have more significant educational opportunities open to them because they are great test-takers. In addition, students often find they are deemed to be better scholastically than their peers if they earn higher scores. Students who learn to employ above-average test-taking skills generally are offered more colligate scholarships. Therefore, it is beneficial for young children to learn how to increase their test-taking skills.

Initially, as soon as their teacher announces a test, third and fourth graders should begin the study and review process. Waiting until a night or two before the test to review can bring heartache and lower grades than anticipated. Numerous third and fourth-grade students will find that they will retain more information when they begin studying days in advance.

I recommend third and fourth graders begin reviewing for tests at least four days prior to the test. Even if they have not been given a review sheet, they should begin their review. Third and fourth graders can start by going back over the bold print or vocabulary words they learned during the unit, such as science, history, social studies, etc.

Next, third and fourth graders benefit from reviewing the assignments that accompanied the unit of study. If they made mistakes on their assignments, they should correct them in order to learn the material accurately. If they are uncertain of the correct answer to a question they missed, they can ask a friend in their class, teacher, a parent or look up the information online. They may wish to write their corrected answer using a colored pencil to help them read it clearer. Third and fourth graders will benefit from correcting the mistakes they made on their graded work.

Each evening the additional test review sessions for third and fourth graders should last for twenty to thirty minutes. If a student has a history of scoring below-average test grades, they can benefit from reviewing forty-five minutes to an hour nightly before the test. The more points students need to add to their test scores, the more extra review and practice time are often required.

Students benefit from being quizzed orally and in written or typed form over the vocabulary words, main concepts, objectives, timelines (if they have them), possible essay questions, and unit quizzes. This technique can significantly assist students in their ability to recall information during a test. It also helps children retain more of the information they need to master.

Students may want to play some games with the test review material to help them have fun while learning. They can benefit from making flashcards of the test review material. Third and fourth graders can use their flashcards to make games to play with family members or friends. The flashcards can also be reviewed while students are being driven to school or riding the school bus. When children have a few extra minutes, they can review their test flashcards. The more students spend time studying and relearning test material, typically, the better they will score on their tests.

In addition, young students need to be prepared that the test questions will often not be asked like they learned the material. Most test question wording is altered, and that rewarding test questions can trip up students to believe nothing they studied was on the test. Therefore, practice with your child orally or in a written form, asking the test information with different wording to help them make the connections between the information they studied and the test questions.

★ Short Answer Test Questions Tip To Help Students Earn Higher Grades

Short answer test questions generally will appear on numerous elementary through college tests. Therefore, students who learn how to answer short answer test questions can have a significant academic advantage over those who struggle with them.

When students find themselves working on the short answer part of the test or quiz, they may freeze up. Many students aren't sure how to answer short answer test questions or even where to begin. Others want to answer essay questions using the least possible words they can. Some will try to answer only using phrases instead of sentences.

One way to help avoid the pitfalls of short answer test questions is to instruct your children to answer the question by restating the main part of the question. When students restate the main question, they often find that they only need to provide a few words from their memory. Students find that this technique provides them with a good beginning for their short answers. It also helps them discover they need to write only a few words in their sentence answer from their memory. This strategy can help lessen the anxiety associated with test-taking. It can also help provide students with a good starting point. As young students learn to restate the questions, many find that they have remembered the correct answer by the time they have to finish their restating.

Cation: If students are having difficulty with their spelling skills, they can self-check their spelling of the short answer with the actual words in the question. This method can help because as the student journeys to higher grade levels, many will find that misspelling can cost them points on their tests.

Third and fourth graders can practice restating the question in their short answer test questions at home. The time students spend practicing test-taking strategies will often provide them with the reward of scoring higher test grades. It also helps students not freeze up while taking tests by providing them a place to begin. If students have experienced test-taking difficulties, the more they can learn about taking a test, the better it often becomes for them. In a world full of tests, young children need not despair and realize that there are ways to learn how to overcome test-taking difficulties and excel in this vital educational area.

December

★ Matching Test Improvement Tips

Young students will find they are faced with matching tests during their elementary and middle school years. Some will encounter matching sections on their tests in high school-level classes. Matching test sections can appear as a more straightforward form of test questions. However, numerous students struggle to excel on the matching part of tests. Some students find these forms to be almost visually overwhelming and extra challenging.

The ability to excel on matching tests is a skill that can be taught to students. Third and fourth graders benefit from being reminded that the wording may be changed or shortened from how it is presented in the classroom learning material. As a result, third and fourth graders can improve their matching test skills by practicing them. Parents or children can make up practice matching tests over the information they will be tested over.

The practice matching tests should be given in three forms. One is the word with the definition or explanation given as it appears in the learning material. The next type should be a shortened version of the information to match with the word. Lastly, the matching practice test should be given with the wording somewhat altered to help students learn to analyze and apply it to vocabulary terms or concepts.

After the third or fourth grader completes the practice matching test, then the parent can help them correct their work. If the student has made mistakes, the parent can analyze the errors to help determine what types of mistakes are being made. Next, students should retake the various forms of practice multiple times until they are able to complete them at the ninety percentile level or higher.

Over the years, I have discovered that making practice matching tests over the material to be learned for the test has helped students learn how to score higher grades on them. The more the student practices taking the three forms of matching tests, the better they can become at taking them. Some students find they are able to go from failing matching tests or test sections to scoring nearly perfect or higher scores. The benefit of practicing how to ace a matching test is numerous test points are added to their scores for many years of their journey to be educated.

Students who have test-taking difficulties benefit from taking parent-made or student-made practice tests to help them score higher grades. This academic solution also can help students who demonstrate test-taking anxieties to be able to overcome them. When students learn they don't have to settle for low or average test scores, they will often feel a sense of relief. The sooner young students learn ways to help them score higher test grades, the better off scholastically they generally are. Tests are a part of the journey to be educated. However, students who struggle in this important area can learn how to excel at test-taking. Students can learn how to overcome their test-taking issues at every grade level and succeed in test-taking.

★ Reading Improvement Quick Tip

As young children study for their end of the semester or quarter tests, they will have countless new terms to memorize. While third and fourth graders are reviewing for the classroom tests, they can also be learning how to read the vocabulary words fluently. Typically, young students will encounter words in their testable information they are unfamiliar with or can't read.

Therefore, an excellent solution to this common reading issue is to help the student learn how to read the words using their phonetic spelling. Writing the phonetic spelling under the word using a colored pencil can help students learn to read them. Then parents should take the time to review the reading of the unfamiliar words with their child. Consistent review of the new words will help young students be able to read them without help.

Students may need to practice reading the words they didn't know how to decode every day until mastery occurs. The constant review of how to read unfamiliar words can help students increase their reading and decoding abilities. Students who spend time re-reading their list of words to be learned can find their reading fluency improving as well. Reading is the process of making sense out of symbols, and the more students work on learning confusing words, the better readers they can become.

★ Because You Asked

> *I am worried about my third-grade daughter's reading level. Her teacher just posted her reading level scores on my daughter's private grades online page. She is reading*

December

at the earlier second-grade level and is more than a year behind. My daughter hasn't participated in any reading program or remediation. Should she work on her reading skills during the winter break or just begin fresh in the New Year?

Thank you for your relevant question. Yes, if a child is reading below grade level or even above their grade level, they will benefit from working on improving their literacy and reading skills over winter break. The average winter break is 16 days long and at least 11 days in most areas. Therefore, winter break is approximately 384 hours, or at the minimum 264 hours long. Utilizing at least 20-30 hours of winter break for reading remediation is an excellent way for students to catch up. Students who are reading below grade level can improve their reading skills before returning to the classroom. Children will discover they still have plenty of time left for family and friends' activities.

Each day children should work on learning a phonetic rule and words that follow the rule per day. They can find phonetic rules online, such as *tion* words. Children should write the phonetic spelling at the top or a paper using a colored pencil. Then they should look for words online, using a dictionary or phonetic workbook from a teacher supply store. Next, they should write the words under the phonetic rule. Students are often very surprised how many words they can learn to read fluently by mastering a phonetic rule.

Next, they can practice reading the word list of words they are unable to decode. The phonetic spelling should be highlighted in each word. This technique can help students retain the phonetic rules. Children will soon find out how much of each word they already know. Then they should review each of their reading lists every day and add a new list to be worked on mastering. Over time students will improve their reading skills by consistent review of their phonetic reading lists.

Additionally, third and fourth graders benefit from reading at several months above their current skill level. Elementary students can improve their reading skills by being challenged to read at several months about their current reading level. This method helps them use their decoding skills to read more challenging material. Moreover, children should read for at a minimum of thirty minutes per day during their winter break. The extra reading work can help propel student's reading levels forward during the second half of the school year.

A fun way to encourage reading is to choose reading material that ties in with the current holiday season. Some students enjoy reading about different holiday celebrations around the world. Learning about other countries' celebrations can also help increase children's knowledge of the world and other cultures. The public library can be an excellent source of children's books about different cultures' celebrations. Seasonal holiday books can make reading time into a fun holiday activity that teaches, improves reading skills, and increases intellectual skills.

★ Dad's Space By Dave Dianis

The holiday season is a great time to play board games with your family that includes using math skills. Board games in which adding, subtracting, and possibly multiplying and dividing scores can be an excellent way to review math skills. The board games can provide fun family time while your children are reinforcing their math skills. Happy December to all!

January

Scholastic Tips To Help Start
The New Year Off Strong

January

The noisemakers have all been blown. The new year has been rung in by now. The bowl games are over, and the holiday parade-lined streets have been cleared of confetti. The cool crisp air reminds third and fourth graders that a new year and semester is here. Half of the school year is over. The school year has now resumed after winter break. Students are returning to their classrooms with a sense of excitement to tell their friends how they spent their time away from school. Even if students lament the ending of their winter break, they generally are refreshed and ready to resume their studies.

Third and fourth grades will soon discover their current curriculum is beginning to move at a much faster pace. The volume, rate, and complexity are steadily reaching the most accelerated levels. Therefore, students benefit from adding an additional ten minutes to their daily student routine to help them keep academic pace with their peers. If ten additional minutes per day isn't enough for a struggling student to excel, add more time. The extra study time can be added in increments of 5 minutes per day until the child is able to catch up scholastically and earn higher grades.

Numerous students will return from school the first days back and claim they don't have to study just yet. They typically describe their desire to ease back into learning and the school routine. However, whether or not a third or fourth grader has homework the first days after school resumes, they should still work on reading, spelling, and review math concepts.

The sooner young students learn to get back into a school routine that includes daily study and homework time, the more they will progress academically. Third and fourth grades don't always realize the value of education. Students tend to try to prolong resuming their study and homework schedule because they don't always see a direct benefit of what they are learning.

Parents may wish to discuss academic goals with their son or daughter the first days back to school. Goal setting early on can help provide students with marks to aim to earn. Third and fourth graders will need a plan to help them achieve their academic goals. Most elementary-aged students are too young to develop an educational program for success that will work for them on an independent level. As a result, third and fourth-grade students benefit from a parent helping them implement a more advanced study plan for the second half of the school year.

Struggling students with average or above-average intelligence can learn how to overcome their learning issues by implementing a proper study and homework routine. Early on in the second half of the school year, students can learn how to succeed in classes, which have challenged them in the past. Starting the second half of the school year off strong can help academically transform lives.

★ Start Fresh In The New Semester

The second half of the school year has now arrived. Third and fourth graders benefit from cleaning out their school binders or start with a new one. Children should file their graded tests and essential papers in file folders to be kept at home. This strategy will help ensure students don't throw out learning material they may still need for class. Parents may need to help their children file and reorganize their school binders.

Students also benefit from being reminded it's a new semester. They are starting a new grading period refreshed. Therefore, they can benefit from setting academic goals in each academic class to work towards achieving. Setting scholastic goals to work toward has helped restore students' motivation. Goal setting can also help increase their effort in the classes they struggle in,

Additionally, school backpacks and lockers should also be cleared out and reorganized to help optimize learning in the new semester. Students also benefit from refreshing their at-home study and supply homework crates. If the pencils, crayons, colored pencils, highlighters, paper, glue, and so on need replacing, this is a great time to do so. The fresh learning materials and reorganized backpacks, notebooks, and lockers can assist students in not becoming bogged down with too much old learning material and items.

Young students also benefit from a desk cleaning and reorganizing any place teachers have for them to store their supplies or work. This technique will help students from having to go on the dreaded search for a book or paper buried in a sea of papers that need to be discarded or filed for later use. This strategy will help save precious time for students. The earlier students can learn to be organized, the better it often is for their academic progress. Additionally, the more organized students appear to their teachers, the higher their instructor's perception of them can be. This visual picture of the children can also help teachers to deem students who demonstrate good organizational skills as higher functioning educationally ones.

The time students spend on improving their organizational skills can have a direct payoff in helping them earn higher grades. Organizational skills can also help speed up the homework and study time process.

★ Organizational Quick Tip For Saving Time On School Mornings

The school morning routine of helping young children make it out of the door to school on time can be easier following one easy strategy. Each evening after the student completes all of their homework and is done studying, they should pack their school backpack or book bag. Then the backpack or book bag should be placed by the door they will be exiting on their way to school.

The backpack or book bag is already packed and just needs to be picked up as they leave for school in the morning. This method helps alleviate a morning search for school items and homework. The student can leave more peaceably for school with all of their work organized in their backpack or book bag waiting at the door. This idea can save much morning anxiety and rushing out the door because they are still loading their school work. Over time students will learn how being more organized is helping to make their school lives easier. Proficient organizational skills can help them earn higher grades for their educational efforts.

★ Math Strategies For Success In The New Year

The third and fourth-grade levels provide the fundamental foundation for math concepts that will be taught at the higher grades. Students who struggle in math at the lower grade levels may continue to have difficulties if they are left un-remediated. Children benefit from starting the new year out practicing the addition, subtraction, multiplication, and division facts for 5 minutes a day. They may want to use triangular flashcards with one number in one corner another in the next one. The answer should be in the last corner.

The reason the triangular flashcards work well is that students can practice the addition and subtraction facts at the same time. They can also review and master the multiplication and division facts simultaneously. Students can practice the facts each day when they have a few extra minutes.

Next, during the weekend, students benefit from pre-learning the math terms, concepts, and formulas they will be introduced to during the upcoming week. Parents or an older sibling can help struggling students practice new formulas and explain terms they seem not to understand. Spending some time pre-learning math concepts during the weekend allows students have some foundational knowledge of the new concepts before the teacher introduces them in class.

The pre-learning helps students have a better understanding of the operations to be learned. This method, in turn, helps students absorb and retain more information during the classroom instructional lessons. Students often find they are grasping a more significant amount of the concepts and feel they are not as confused with what the teacher demonstrates to the class.

Math challenged children, when they do their math homework, benefit from having a parent check their work after they complete three problems. The reason for this is if they are making mistakes, they can be catch and retaught before they spend too much time completing their work inaccurately. Then the parent can reteach the operation and repeat the process until the math homework is done for the evening.

After the math homework is finished, students benefit from looking over the concepts, formulas, and terms they will be introduced to in the next day's class. Again, the time third and fourth graders spend pre-learning the math lessons can bring significant payoffs in mastery and grades. Students who have struggled in math can learn how to overcome their math challenges. Additionally, they will often have a great degree of academic success in their math classes as they continue their education.

★ Science Tips For Better Grades

As children have already discovered, science is an integral part of *STEM* classes. The study of science is now being emphasized more and more. The school curriculums are teaching science classes at a more demanding level than past generations. The academic focus on science classes can leave the scientifically challenged students scholastically behind their peers.

The good news is that there are proven methods and techniques that can transform scientifically challenged students into earning higher grades. The sooner third and fourth-grade students catch up and learn they can excel in this area of study, the better it is for them.

First, students benefit from pre-reading their assigned reading material before they are taught it in class. Students may wish to only pre-read the pages that will be taught the next day in school. Then they should spend time reading the bold print words with their definition and explanation. Next, they should read any process or formula such as photosynthesis three to four times before they are introduced in class. Then if the student is confused over any of the concepts, terms, or processes, they should ask their parent or older sibling for extra help.

If they are still confused, they should consult a dictionary or online academic source for a more complete explanation. Typically, the Internet will provide students with a more visual description of the same factual information. Pictures can help visual children with a more concrete explanation. Then they should return to their text, online classroom source, or teacher-provided reading material and test their understanding. If they are still struggling to understand one or more concepts, they can jot down questions to ask their teacher during the lesson.

After the lesson has been taught and the students are working on their homework, parents should reread the assigned reading with them. Students benefit from reading their assigned reading three and four times to help them fill in learning gaps. Children will notice that they will pick up new information they missed in the past readings each time they read their scientific material. If a child balks at the multiple reading system, then remind them that every time someone sees the same movie or show, they pick up details they missed the initial time.

As the third or fourth grader works through their lessons from their unit of study parents should question and quiz their son or daughter to make sure they are mastering all of the material. When parents deem there are concepts, formulas, or processes that need additional work, they can make notes over the ideas that still need further work. Parents can help struggling students review and relearn the tricky concepts, formulas, or processes before they are tested over them.

In addition, as parents look over their child's graded science assignments and find missed questions, they can help them correct their work. Correcting missed items help students relearn and refresh their understanding of scientific material.

★ Because You Asked

> *January always seems to be a long month after the holiday season has ended. The fall sports are over, and my son has more time to devote to his reading skills. He is in the third grade and is several months behind in his reading skills. I am worried that he is digressing in his reading because he was reading at grade level in the last few school years. My son has not begun any remedial reading programs and has difficulty decoding multi-syllable words. What do you recommend he do to help him remediate his reading and be able to read at third-grade level standards?*

Thank you for your relevant question about your son's reading skills. The ability to read on or above grade level is extremely important in a child's journey to be educated. If reading and decoding multi-syllable words are cause your son to fall behind, there are some remedial activities to help him improve in his reading.

Multi-syllable words are constructed mainly by adding affixes to base words at the elementary school level. When your son encounters multi-syllable words while reading, ask him to locate the base word within the larger word. Then point out that within most multi-syllable words is a base word with suffixes and or prefixes added to them.

Next, record the suffixes and prefixes he seems to be misreading or unable to recognize. Then take the affix list and work on teaching up to ten at a time. Write the prefix or suffix on notebook paper and make a running reading list to go over every day until he masters them.

Subsequently, when your son is reading and encounters multi-syllable words, which include affixes, help him identify them in the words. Then help him locate words in his assigned reading material with the affixes he is learning in them. Next, ask him to decode the words by locating the base word and then adding the affixes. Then ask your son to read the entire word three times before moving on to the following words.

Over time by learning to read affixes, your son can improve his ability to read, decode and blend multi-syllable words. You may be amazed at the tremendous improvement he can make in his reading skills. Children can learn how to become great readers!

★ Mom's Space By Karen Dianis

The holiday season has ended, and the noisemakers ushering another year have been discarded. Young students are returning to school with exciting stories of how they spent their time away. January is a good month to spend several minutes a day designing a holiday memory book. Students can place pictures of their time with family and friends in a creative way. They can practice their sentence writing skills by writing a descriptive sentence to describe each of their special pictures.

The creative sentences they work on to describe each picture can help them improve their written language skills. They can use creative and entertaining words to retell what is happening in each picture they place in their memory book. The holiday memory book can be a fantastic way to preserve fun family's and friends' memories of the special times they spent together. It can also help students learn how to write impressive descriptive sentences while having a fun time. Happy January to all!

February

Learning Strategies To Help Bring Academic Achievement

February

Visions of pink, red and white hearts have taken their yearly place in classrooms and stores. The hearts serve as a reminder for children and adults to treat everyone with kindness and respect. The cutout hearts are a nice way to help young children know that their family and friends love them.

Young children's classrooms also have bulletin boards with pictures of past presidents and other famous people. Soon students will be learning more about our country's history and the people who helped build a nation. The shortened month of February is one filled with exceptional historical learning. However, numerous third and fourth graders are focused on the idea that soon, they will have a few days of vacation from school.

February is also the month that will be packed with new learning. The curriculum will continue to accelerate toward its fastest pace. The volume and complexity of the school year are revving up to their highest rate. Third and fourth graders should add an additional five minutes or more to each class study schedule; they are scoring average to low average marks at the end of the grading period. Students can learn how to excel in their academic classes.

★ February Communication Tip

The second month of the new semester is an excellent time for parents to check in with their third or fourth grader's teacher(s). The communication can be as simple as emailing your child's teacher(s) to double-check if your son or daughter has any academic areas that they are falling behind in. A proactive parent can help eliminate potential scholastic glitches before they become academic problems.

The sooner academic glitches or problems are addressed and worked on at home to remediate, the better the outcome generally is for the student. Parents, please remember that young students typically are not able to fix their academic issues on their own. The reason is they often lack the ability to be able to design and follow an educational plan to remediate their weaknesses.

However, many students may only require several days of remedial work to effectively understand a troublesome scholastic concept. Parents who spend some additional time re-explaining confusing learning material to their students can prevent them from developing learning gaps. Communication with the classroom teacher can dramatically assist parents in knowing what concepts should be remediated. Waiting until the parent-teacher spring conference can be almost too late for quick remediation.

Communication with your child's classroom teacher (s) can have a tremendous effect on their ability to keep scholastic pace with their peers. Communication between parents and their child's teacher (s) can help prevent learning gaps from becoming educational challenges. Additionally, students who have a parent that communicates with their child's school are less likely to drop out of school, according to the *Graham study of 2006*.

★ Reading Comprehension Tips To Help Increase Skills

Students will often read a paragraph, page, or chapter with very little memory of what they read. They find it challenging to recall relevant details of the text or assigned reading material. One of the reasons young students may have difficulties retaining what they read is that they are so focused on decoding the words they forget to pay attention to the meaning of the text. Others may find their minds are focused elsewhere and not concentrating on the text. For some, it is a combination of both.

The good news is that third and fourth-grade students can learn how to read and retain the important information from their assigned reading. One proven solution is to ask your child to read a paragraph then write down two concepts they remembered in the paragraph. The ideas can be one or more phrases or one word to represent the information. If they cannot retain one or more concepts, they should reread the paragraph before proceeding to the next one.

Some students may have to write a remembered word or phrase after reading one or two sentences until they can read an entire paragraph and retain the information. This technique generally works because children are aware, they must convey one to three ideas per paragraph before moving on to the next one. The students tend to learn how to keep their minds on what they are reading. They also learn that they not only have to read the words, but they must focus on the content of the text.

Over time students can learn how to help themselves learn not only to read the words but to retain the essential details. Parents can assist their students by asking them to verbally answer comprehension questions that work on the who, what, when, how, and action of the reading. This technique has aided countless students with reading comprehension issues in overcoming their weaknesses. Students who learn how to comprehend the contextual meaning of their assigned reading can become academic achievers.

★ Spelling Improvement Techniques

Third and fourth graders who experience spelling difficulties can learn how to become proficient spellers. Each week students generally are given a weekly spelling list to learn. On Friday, the spelling test is given to determine mastery of the words. Numerous students demonstrate problems with learning the words and passing the weekly test.

The good news is that students can learn how to master their classroom weekly spelling tests. First, students should look over the new list and highlight the vowel spelling found in each of the words using a consistent color. Then they should separate all of the sight words that may be on their list. The sight words are words that don't follow any phonetic rule and have to be memorized. Next, they should have a parent or friend give them a pretest over the words to determine what words they may already know. It will also tell them what part of each misspelled word they did spell correctly.

Next, students benefit from highlighting the part of the word or letters in each of the words they misspelled. Then they should highlight in another color the letters in each word they spelled correctly. Then the number of letters they need to learn in each word should be placed beside the incorrect spelling. Students may find they are surprised when they determine there are phonetic parts of each spelling word they already know.

Then students should spend time taking each spelling word and saying the spelling letter by letter in a recording. The words can be recorded on a cell phone, computer, or tape recorder. Students can use their recording of each spelling word to reinforce the information by listening and spelling the words along with their recording.

Children benefit from writing the letters of each word on paper as they listen to them on their recordings. They may even wish to make spelling chants for each letter in their recording to add some rhythm to aid their memory.

Each homework and study day, students should listen to their recording and write the words along with their recording three or four times. Next, they should take a practice test to help them determine which words they have learned. This method will allow the students to focus on the words that still need additional work to master.

Then third and fourth graders should write the misspelled words correctly several times a day. While they are spelling the words and looking at the correct spelling, they should say aloud the letters they are writing to provide them with additional reinforcement.

Third and fourth grades should place cards with the correct spelling of each word they find troublesome in various places they often see around their home. Each time they see their spelling card, they should spell the word five times orally. This strategy will provide students with extra practice.

These activities should be done in concert with their classroom spelling assignments. By Wednesday evening, students should have learned most of the words. They should then zero in on the words that are still tricky for them.

Numerous third and fourth grades benefit from spelling the weekly spelling words they find troublesome with plastic or cutout letters. Spelling the words using manipulatives such as plastic letters has helped numerous students learn their weekly spelling words. Many students find learning the spelling words more enjoyable when using cutout or plastic letters to spell the words and correct misspelling.

In addition, the use of cutout or plastic letters to practice troublesome spelling words provides the student with more visual and kinesthetic information to aid the brain's retention ability. Parents may find that their student complains less about studying their spelling words when fun manipulatives are used for their review time. Spelling-challenged students can learn how to become proficient spellers.

★ Reading Improvement Quick Tip

Reading at or above grade level standards can be challenging for more than half of the student population in the United States. It is shocking to realize that most students will struggle with reading during their academic years. However, reading is one of the most essential skills for students to master. Whether or not a student has been diagnosed with Dyslexia or is just experiencing challenges in their reading ability, they can be helped.

When students are presented with their classroom's weekly spelling list, they can use the words and their derivatives to learn more reading words. Each week most students will be presented with at a minimum of twenty new words to learn. Most of the words on their classroom's spelling list will have other words that are derivatives of them.

An example of a word with derivatives is a nation: national, nationalistic, nationalism, alienation, alternation, carbonation, destination, explanation, fascination, and so on. There are approximately 437 English words that contain the word nation in them. Students can choose from five to twenty words that are derivatives of several of their spelling words to learn to master when reading.

It is beneficial for young students to be taught the concept of words being part of numerous other words. The derivative technique can help young children master more reading words and at a faster rate. The reason is students already know a larger part of the word they are reading and just need to learn the added letters and blend them together to read other words.

Students with Dyslexia or Dyslexic tendencies can dramatically benefit from learning how to read words that are made of derivatives. Students with reading disabilities can be taught this method to help them overcome and master their reading challenges. Moreover, they benefit from reviewing their self-made or parent-made reading lists of derivatives until complete mastery is made.

The derivative reading technique can open up a whole list of numerous words that coincide with the words they are learning. Young students generally have fun locating are reading words that are derivatives of their spelling words. The derivatives of their spelling words can be found online, on a cell phone, or in a dictionary. Some spelling workbooks with provide students with some derivatives for their spelling words. Children can learn how to accelerate their reading skills when learning their classroom's weekly spelling words.

★ Math Improvement Quick Tip

Math is becoming an essential class as STEM classes seem to be the trend of the future. Schools are focused on math skills, and many have accelerated their curriculum pace and volume of the mathematics classes. Math can be a very troublesome class for numerous right-brain-thinking students. Countless young students complain that they are just beginning to understand a mathematical procedure, and then the class moves on to new material.

Elementary students may find they are falling behind in math because they haven't totally mastered one concept before moving on to another. Most math-challenged students find themselves perplexed on how to remediate their math skills.

To help remedy math issues, students benefit from practicing and reviewing math procedures previously learned this school year. After school, each day, students should review and practice one or two math problems, which review prior taught concepts. The reason for this is math builds upon itself. Math gaps or unmastered procedures can lead students to demonstrate further mathematical struggles.

Students who faithfully review and practice previously taught math concepts and procedures benefit from the consistent work to master them. Elementary-age students are generally flabbergasted to discover that reviewing and practicing prior introduced math concepts need only to take them a few extra minutes a day.

The student's math textbook, graded assignments, or online math source are good sources to locate problems and concepts to review. Parents can write down one or two problems for their students to solve. If your son or daughter struggles to remember how to solve the problems, then review the procedure(s) with them.

When they finish solving the problem or problems, then go over their work with them and check it for mastery. Next, if they have made a mistake, then work with your student to correct their calculations. When students demonstrate they are still struggling to learn one or more concepts, these troublesome ones should be reviewed daily until mastery occurs. The consistent review will benefit students, and over time, mastery generally happens.

If your son or daughter complains about practicing and reviewing previously taught mathematical concepts, they need to be let in on some practical advice. The reluctant student can benefit from learning that math builds upon itself. Therefore, misunderstood concepts and unmastered math procedures can lead them into further mathematical challenges as they continue their journey to be educated.

A student may need further encouragement to practice prior taught math material. They may need to be enlightened to the idea that when they become more proficient in math, they will save themselves time and frustration in their future math classes. The time they can save themselves in the future can be

February

used in other ways than having to relearn math concepts from their past. Some high school mathematical challenged students can trace their math gaps to unmastered material from their elementary school classes. Higher grade level students who have to relearn concepts from their past often find their math gaps are lessened by relearned unmastered procedures. Students can learn how to become proficient math students!

★ Because You Asked

> *My fourth-grade daughter has zero interest in math and, as a result, is barely passing her math class. I have tried talking to her about working harder in her math class, but that doesn't seem to help. Do you have any suggestions to help her learn to like math class and raise her low grades?*

Thank you for your question regarding your daughter and her apparent dislike for math. The scenario you are facing with your daughter is a common one among students. Numerous students feel adversely toward math. Generally, when students demonstrate negative feelings toward their mathematics class, they believe they're not talented in the area of study.

The good news is that students can learn how to overcome their math challenges and succeed in math class. First, please explain to your daughter that the world is full of math. Then ask her to practice the basic math facts until she is able to recall them in a few seconds each. She may need to practice the addition, subtraction, multiplication, and division facts for fifteen minutes daily until she becomes more proficient in them.

Next, she needs to learn the vocabulary of math, which was addressed in the past months. Then she should practice each math procedure she is learning each day for about fifteen to twenty minutes and correct her mistakes using a colored pencil.

Then ask her to help you calculate various amounts, such as how much the grocery bill will be for the week. Then she can add each grocery receipt to calculate how much was spent on groceries for the month and so on. She can also benefit from calculating items that are on sale and how much the discount is. Your daughter can also learn to determine how much a sale item will cost after the sale price is subtracted from the regular price.

Everyday household math calculations such as how much an electric bill changed from one month to another can help her improve her math skills. Children benefit from having math problems presented to them to calculate can help improve their confidence and academic self-esteem. In addition, this technique will help show her the importance of math and how it is used in peoples' daily lives.

★ Dad's Space By Dave Dianis

My daughter didn't enjoy math when she was in elementary and middle school. She didn't see a need to learn math and would have preferred a curriculum devoid of math. However, I taught her how to calculate the amount of several items she wished to own from the local store on an online vendor. Then we worked through if the items were cheaper at a store or online. We then worked out how much extra shipping costs added to the final costs.

Most of the calculations we would do together took several steps to be able to come up with the amount. The several-step problems taught her how to figure out how to break down problems into steps and solve each step to find an answer. Over time she began to improve in her math skills and learned to see the value of math. Her attitude toward math improved along with her skills. This technique became a fun activity we could do together. Happy February to all!

March

Academic Guidance For Scholastic Achievement

March

As the snow falls lessen and the ground melts into spring, third and fourth graders are reaching for lighter jackets. Their thoughts are turning toward the anticipation of warmer days and time spent outside with friends. Spring sports are beaconing children to participate and become team members. Spring break will soon be here. Children can hardly wait to have a week away from school, and some deserved freedom from the school schedule.

The calendar turns from February to March also signifies the most academically demanding pace and volume is now upon young students. The academic curriculum is accelerating weekly to its swiftest pace. Even with Spring Break, the month of March is jammed packed with new learning concepts. Young students may find they are experiencing difficulty keeping up the educational pace with their peers. Even children who have excelled academically in all their subjects may find themselves falling behind for the first time.

Therefore, if a third or fourth grader is falling behind or struggling to master the new learning concepts, additional time should be added to their daily study routine. Students need not despair the increases in study time need to apply only to their troublesome classes. Children benefit from adding ten minutes per difficult subject area per day. If your student protests the new study schedule, remind him or her that school will be over for the year in a few months.

Children benefit from being reminded that school curriculums spiral around. If students don't master learning material at the current grade level, it may cause scholastic difficulties later on for them. The sooner learning glitches, gaps, or diagnosed problems are remediated, the better it generally is for the child. It is typically easier to master unmastered learning concepts at the lower grades than it is at the high-grade levels.

★ March Written Language Strategies For Skill Improvement

The academic skills of written language are one of the most complex. It is at the highest levels of academic learning. Students typically express that they don't know what to write or where to begin when writing assignments are given. Whether the task calls for creative sentences, paragraphs, or report writing, there are fun and effective ways to help students become impressive writers.

When third and fourth graders are assigned a written language task, they often declare they aren't sure where to begin. Students may procrastinate and use avoidance strategies to prolong their start time. Written language-challenged students benefit from reading their assignment several times and brainstorming their sentences prior to beginning. Third and fourth grades are often surprised to figure out that brainstorming ideas can lessen the time they spend on completing their task in an impressive manner.

Students should also have access to a list of impressive words, such as ones in a junior-level thesaurus. The more difficult words should replace several common ones per sentence they write. However, a caution, students should look up the meaning of the words they use to substitute common ones. The new words need to be suitable synonyms for the common ones. It is not unusual for children to choose words that don't really match the true meaning of the basic ones they are trying to substitute.

The writing technique of substituting common words such as gigantic or colossal instead of big or large can help students improve their written language skills. This technique is one that students can tremendously benefit from throughout their academic years. The student should choose one to two words per sentence to substitute common words with impressive descriptive words.

As students look up common words to find impressive ones, they benefit from reading the definition of several of the word choices. This method can help them have a broader vocabulary to use in their written language assignments and speech. Third and fourth grades who use higher-level vocabulary in their writing and speech will often appear more intelligent to their peers and teachers.

When students are writing a creative writing paragraph or report, they can benefit from accurately substituting five to eight common words per paragraph with impressive ones. Even if third and fourth-grade students are writing sentences with their weekly spelling words, this can help them score higher grades.

After students have substituted common words for more impressive ones, they should reread their sentences aloud to help them check for flow and clarity. Students who learn early on in their educational journey to self-edit and check for flow and clearly stated sentences and paragraphs generally become better writers. Third and fourth graders can learn how to write impressive sentences and paragraphs.

★ Vocabulary Skills Improvement Quick Tip

Third and fourth graders are generally at the early stages of learning to correctly use vocabulary words in their speech and writing assignments. Students who have a high-level working vocabulary for their spoken words and writing often appear to be brighter than their common word using peers. Even if a student has a diagnosed learning issue such as Dyslexia, ADD, or Language Learning Disability, they can learn how to employ high-level vocabulary words in their speech and writing.

Elementary students benefit from learning the meaning and correct use of three to five words per week they are unfamiliar with and have yet to master. They can choose the vocabulary words to learn from their textbooks, online learning sources, or a junior or regular dictionary. Students can write down the three to five words to learn on paper with their definitions. They should include a sentence from their vocabulary source that correctly uses the word in a sentence. This technique can be done on Sundays before the start of a new school week. Then each day after school, students should work on learning how to read the word, its definition and how to use it correctly in a sentence. As each school week begins to reach mid-week, they should be orally quizzed over their three to five words by a parent.

Next, during mealtime, each day, or regular conversations, third and fourth graders should use their vocabulary words in sentences when conversing with a parent. If they misuse one or more words, they should be corrected by a parent or older sibling. Next, they should work on relearning the meaning of the word. Then students benefit from correctly using it in verbal sentences. Before long, third and fourth graders can improve their language vocabulary skills by several grade levels.

★ Math Quick Tip For Word Problems Improvement

Today's modern math curriculums include an increased emphasis on solving complex math word or story problems. These types of math problems cause countless students anxiety because they can be very challenging to work out. Additionally, many new mathematical word problems require young students to write out their answers in words and numbers. Writing out solutions to word problems in sentence form has become a growing trend in the United States.

First, ask your student to read the word or story problem three times before attempting to answer the question. The three read-throughs will assist struggling students in locating the main "do" words. Then the student can lightly cross through extra information which is not relevant for solving the problem.

This method will help them not to focus on irrelevant details and focus on the actual problem.

Next, struggling students can dramatically benefit from writing on a piece of paper the numbers that are needed to solve the word or story problem. Then they should write the mathematical signs which are found in the word problem. Generally, the math signs will be written in words such as addends to represent to add.

Once the numbers and signs are written separate from the word problem, the struggling student should reread the word problem. Next, they should place the numbers in order of the operations needed to solve the story question. Next, the student adds the mathematical signs the equation demands.

The student should work on solving the numeric problem found in the word problem. After self-checking their work by working the problem backward, they are ready to write out their answer in words.

Many struggling students are unsure how to write their answer to a story problem in sentence form. Children can benefit from rewriting the "do" part of the word problem in their answer. This strategy will help them be able to write a complete solution in written form to the math problem.

Students often find this technique can dramatically help them be able to solve and answer story the dreaded word problems accurately. The more proficient third and fourth graders becoming at solving word problems and writing out their answers in sentence form, the higher their math grades can become. Struggling math students can learn how to become great learners!

★ Science Improvement Techniques

As the STEM classes are becoming increasingly more vital for young students to learn how to shine in, they often find themselves struggling to learn new concepts. Typically, by the second semester, scientific concepts are being introduced at a steady and swifter pace. Some children will find themselves struggling to keep up with their classroom expectations.

Therefore, students generally can dramatically improve their ability to learn and demonstrate their knowledge of scientific concepts by implementing proven strategies. First, prior to a new unit being introduced, peruse the online or textbook chapter with your child. Then go over all of the formulas, pictures, diagrams, and bold print with your student. Re-read all of the important information listed in the last sentences several times with your child.

Next, if there are bold print scientific words such as fibrous roots or tap roots, which can be demonstrated with visual aids, please provide them. If the concept is the difference between a physical change or a chemical change, that can be easily demonstrated. The visual aids can be introduced as the students learn each section in class. The visual aids can dramatically help students learn and retain scientific concepts.

Then during the earlier days of the scientific unit, ask your child to either act out or draw the scientific terms or concepts. Teaching students to act out of the scientific concepts or show them hand gestures to represent the concept, such as the steps of photosynthesis, assists retention of scientific learning. The actions or gestures can help students retain and recall more scientific information.

Students who review scientific concepts by drawing them or acting them out with actions or hand gestures generally perform better on their tests and quizzes. The additional visual aids to demonstrate new science terms or concepts can have a pronounced effect on student's ability to master science at the third and fourth-grade level. Students generally find they are enjoying learning about science more; their understanding increases so does their interest. Science classes can be manageable and mastered!

★ Because You Asked

> *My fourth grader is falling behind in his reading and reading comprehension skills. He is telling me that he will take the entire week of Spring Break off from school work. Do you think that is a good idea, or should he do some remedial work during his week away from school?*

Thank you for your pertinent question. Spring Break and possible school remedial work have been a source of contention for numerous students and their parents. First, your son appears to be falling behind in his reading and reading comprehension skills. Therefore, an entire week away from all reading or reading comprehension work may not be to his best advantage academically speaking.

As an Educational Specialist, I understand students' need to clear their minds from school and take a break. However, if a student is falling behind in one or more academic subject areas, they can benefit from incorporating an hour a day for academic remediation. Spring Break is typically a time when students are not given additional school work.

Therefore, dedicating an hour a day to reading and reading comprehension improvement can help students stay on track and possibly improve their skills. Divide the hour in half and designate one-half to read and the other to reading comprehension skills. The reading remediation can be working on learning words from his grade level reading that he demonstrates difficulty mastering.

Ask your son to work on with you or another family member the words he seems to have difficulty learning to read. Create a reading list of difficult words from reading with him and help him remember them over the week. Next, ask him to bring home his reader before the break or use his online source to read ahead and work on answering comprehension questions at the end of the story. If the story doesn't have any comprehension questions, then create five to seven of them.

Over the week of Spring Break, many students find that working on their scholastic skills for an hour a day helps them be sharper academically when school resumes. The additional time can also assist students in restoring educational self-esteem. Remember, your son will have plenty of time left over to do other activities during Spring Break.

★ Mom's Space By Karen Dianis

The month of March can be a wonderful one to help students become more organized students. At the beginning of each week, ask your child to reorganize his or her notebook, file folders, study supplies, and backpack. The weekly reorganization can help prevent the final months of the school year from becoming less organized because of increasing curriculum demands and more activities.

For each week your child re-organizes their school belongings, you may allow your student to choose a chore they can skip for the week. Many children are motivated by being rewarded with picking one chore they can omit for one evening or day. Happy March to all!

April

Learning Strategies To Promote Success In School

April

The fresh spring air is filled with the smells of the earth renewing itself. April showers bring the hues of spring green and beautiful flowers to life. The longer days and warmer temperatures are calling children outdoors. Spring sports have geared up, and children's minds are starting to drift toward summer vacation. Now is the time for elementary students to work toward finishing the school year off strong.

The month of April's learning strategies can help make it possible for struggling students to transform their learning weaknesses and become academically high-achieving pupils. Moreover, students will experience the curriculum accelerating at a swift and steady pace. They will often find the units of study in their core classes will be presented faster. The unit tests will typically become closer together as the year begins winding down.

The good news for third and fourth graders is they can add a few minutes of additional study and review time to their current routine to help them keep pace with their peers. The extra five to ten minutes can be the initial step to help them transform their grades. This strategy will also help them overcome their academic weaknesses.

If your child balks over adding a few extra minutes to their study time, then you may want to remind him or her how many weeks of school remain until summer break. Also, you may find adding some review time during the weekends can help struggling students learn how they can overcome their scholastic weaknesses. April can be a month of academic success for struggling students.

★ Reading Improvement Strategies For Success

Third and fourth-grade students can learn how to overcome reading issues and excel in their skills. In the month of April, elementary school students will be presented with numerous multi-syllable words in their classroom reading teaching sources. Whether their class reader is an actual book or online source, this next strategy can help improve their reading skills.

Before a new reading story is taught in your child's reading instructional class, you should pre-read the story with your child. When your third or fourth grader finds a word, they are unable to read, blend or decode write the word down on paper. Go over the word with your child and show them how to blend the word.

Then ask your child to continue to read until they find the next troublesome word. Write down and review every word your elementary-age student demonstrates difficulty reading. After the story is read in its entirety, go over the list of unmastered words with your daughter or son.

Next, look up the phonetic pronunciation and write it next to each word on their list. Please go over the troublesome word list with your child and help her or him use the phonetic pronunciation to read the words. Then in the morning, prior to the story being introduced in their classroom lessons, go over the words again. The list with the phonetic spelling by the words should be copied to have one for school and one for home. The list can serve as an excellent instructional tool during your child's reading class.

Every day during study and homework time, go over the reading list with your child. Also, spend time re-reading the story with your son or daughter. If he or she continues to struggle reading, blending, or decoding the word, then go over the missed words again.

Parents may want to put a small checkmark by the words their student is able to read from the list without decoding or blending. As each word is mastered during the several days the reading story is being read in class, please make a big deal out of your child's accomplishment. Then repeat this process prior to a new reading story being introduced in their classroom.

During the weekends, the reading list should be gone over and re-read several times a day. As mastery occurs, then the list of mastered words only needs to be reviewed every so often for retention to occur. As each list is mastered, you may wish to reward them with a small reward for their additional effort. The small rewards can help motivate students to work through scholastic skills that are difficult for them. Remember, students respond to positive praise and or small rewards for the work. Students can learn how to overcome their reading issues and become skilled readers.

★ Reading Comprehension Improvement Tips

The ability to retain and understand what one reads is one of the most important scholastic skills. Students who are behind their grade-level expectations in reading comprehension should work on rebuilding their skills on a daily basis. Even if your daughter or son is receiving remedial help, they should still be working at home to improve these vital learning skills.

April

Every school day, students with reading comprehension challenges should work at home toward strengthening these skills. One proven method that has helped countless students progress in their reading comprehension is the read and discuss method. Students can dramatically benefit from employing this technique when working on their assignments.

While reading their assigned homework, third and fourth graders should read each paragraph with a parent, sibling, or friend. After each paragraph is read, they should be discussed, and several key points should be gone over. If the student reads the paragraph and is unable to retain the key points, then the discussions should take place after one-half of the paragraph is read. If one-half is too much, then the paragraph can be broken down into quartiles.

The key points should be gone over directly after the section of the reading has been read. If the child focuses on the less relevant facts, then the more essential points should be pointed out to her or him. Then the next paragraph should be read, and the process of immediate discussions should be done.

After a time, this technique can help students to heighten their ability to focus on the meaning of the text. Students generally find they are soon learning how to zero in on the key points and retain them.

When the third or fourth grader has mastered reading one paragraph and then discuss, they can read more of the text before stopping. The goal is for students to be able to read half of a page to an entire page and retain the main points.

After the student has completed the entire reading assignment, they should discuss all of the main points with their reading partner. Over time students typically discover they are able to increase their reading comprehension skills. They can often read, retain, understand, and access the new information they read in the assignments faster.

This technique also helps students from focusing on information that is not as important as the main facts. Students can learn how to have strong reading comprehension skills. They can also learn how to become more focused during their assigned reading time!

★ Spring Spelling Tips For Success

April spelling lists usually include more multi-syllable words than ones from the winter lists. Now that the final months of school are here, educators add more difficult words to their classroom's weekly spelling lists. Therefore, students with spelling issues can benefit from adding some new techniques to help them learn how to succeed in spelling.

Generally, students with spelling problems become visually overwhelmed looking at the lists. The sense of anxiety can exacerbate difficulties in learning weekly spelling lists. However, students can learn how to break down spelling words into manageable parts for mastery.

As soon as a child receives their classroom's weekly spelling list, the words should be gone over with the student. A parent should go over each of the words and help the child look for phonetic rules in each word. Then, they should highlight the parts of each of the words the student doesn't know how to spell. Generally, each word will contain letters that the student can spell without help. The highlighted part of the word helps students zero in on the part(s) of the word they need to learn.

Next, the parent can help their student by taking the word and pronouncing it how it looks like it should be said by the spelling. An example of this is the word fabulous can be for the purposes of learning as fab-ul-long o- us. This technique is relatively easy and helps the student learn a way to retain the spelling and simplify it. Each troublesome word should be divided into parts that sound like the word is spelled, not necessarily pronounced. Providing a spelling-challenged student with the auditory tools such as learning to spell the word by how they look like they would be pronounced can help mastery. It also helps students when they are taking their spelling tests in class to have a memory hook to help them spell the words correctly by saying the words as they appear; they should be spelled. Another example is the word should. It looks like it would be read as sh long o long u and ld. It can be learned for spelling as sh o u ld.

Then when the child is learning their weekly spelling list, they can say the word to themselves that matches the spelling. This technique provides students with hooks and tools to help trigger their spelling memory. When students employ this strategy, they often discover learning they become more proficient spellers. As students learn how to apply spelling strategies to their weekly spelling words, they can find it easier to pass the tests. Children also generally find they are able to retain the spelling of the words and truly master them. Third and fourth grades who struggle in the area of spelling can learn how to become fantastic spellers and score higher grades as a result.

April

★ **Punctuation Help**

In today's curriculums, grammar and punctuation instruction have dramatically lessened in importance. Even though numerous school systems have limited time spent teaching correct grammar and punctuation, these skills are still relevant to modern students.

The ability to correctly punctuate one's sentences, paragraphs and written assignments still have relevance to students. It seems almost contradictory that numerous students are penalized and points deducted on assignments for punctuation mistakes. Making students accountable to know the rules is especially difficult when English classes have been almost swept from the curriculum.

The good news is struggling students can learn how to self-check their use of punctuation and prevent themselves from losing valuable points. First, ask third and fourth graders to self-check their sentences for beginning and ending punctuation marks. Students of all grade levels. Forfeit points for omitting capitalization and sentence-ending marks. Children can learn how to check each sentence for the basics.

Next, children can learn the comma rules by downloading a list of them. Then they can practice applying them to their written work. Using commons in a list is relatively easy for students to learn. The who/which clause rule of using a comma after those words in a sentence can be mastered quickly. The beginning of a sentence with an interjection is not as challenging to master. There are approximately 13 comma rules for students to master. Students may find they can retain the comma rules by learning them over 13 weeks. The comma rules can be tricky, but their points on graded assignments can increase when the basic ones are applied.

Third and fourth graders can also learn how to correctly use quotation marks in sentences that contain words people are speaking. The idea of checking their sentences that have quotations with a left -hand then the right-hand movement can serve as a self-checking tool.

Elementary school children can benefit from practicing adding correct punctuation to sentences a parent makes up for them. Practice sentences can also be found online that are designed for third and fourth grades to apply the punctuation rules. Students may wish to use colored pencils for each type of punctuation mark. The color pencils can add interest and serve as a visual reminder of the rules. Children can benefit from practicing adding correct punctuation rules to three or four sentences daily.

Another fun way to practice punctuation rules is for the child to make a poster or several posters for their room. On the poster(s), the 13 main comma rules can be illustrated or represented in words and pictures. They can then add the rules for beginning and ending marks. The quotation rules should be added as well. Students can look online for all of the primary third and fourth-grade punctuation rules. The student-made posters can provide students with daily reminders of punctuation rules that should be mastered.

Third and fourth graders that master basic punctuation rules can help themselves earn higher grades on their assignments, quizzes, tests, and future exams. The ability to apply punctuation rules can also help them succeed in their future workplace.

★ Grammar Improvement Help

Grammar and English classes can be confusing to numerous elementary students. Learning a grammar rule in isolation can assist children in their mastery of them. The eight parts of speech that are typically taught to third and fourth grades can be tricky to learn. One way to help students understand them is to find a poster for their room that contains the eight parts of speech. The poster can serve as a daily reminder of the main grammar rules. Students who see and read the grammar poster can learn and retain the grammar rules without spending hours and hours learning them.

There are some fun cartoon-type books available online, or the local public library may have them. They are a fun way to read and teach elementary-level students grammar rules. The funny illustrations help keep children interested and entertained while learning valuable knowledge. The grammar cartoon books generally contain practice sentences to help students master them. Elementary-age students should read the grammar cartoon booklets each week to help them gain complete mastery.

Elementary students can also improve their grammar skills by designing pictures to post in their rooms of the parts of speech. Each illustration should contain one to three of the parts of speech. The images should be placed on construction paper. The pictures can be taken from a cell phone or found online, or drawn. Then each part of speech should be labeled above the pictures

April

that will provide pictorial examples. Next, students can make up sentences to describe the part of speech for each picture. An example of this is a picture of a beach. The student can underline all of the words that are nouns in their descriptive sentence. They can also circle all of the pictures on nouns in their photograph, online source, or drawing. The adverbs or adjectives can be writing by each verb or noun on the illustrations.

Third and fourth graders should include the definition of each of the parts of speech in each picture. The pictures typically serve multiple purposes. They can be an excellent and fun way to practice and learn the parts of speech. The pictures can also be posted in their child's room to provide visual reinforcement and reminders to help improve their mastery. In addition, children can discover that learning can be fun and made easier when worked on over time. Students can learn to master grammar concepts and have a fun time while learning new skills!

★ Map Skills Quick Tip

Young students will be instructed to learn where the fifty states, continents, oceans, seas, countries, large cities, main waterways are on the world map. They may only be required to learn some of the above information during the third and fourth grade school years. However, elementary students can use the following techniques to help themselves learn the map. These methods can be used at every grade level.

First, there are map skills game sites on the internet that quiz map skills of certain chosen areas. Most of the map skill sites will have a menu of the area for the student to select from a list. Map skill games can help students learn how to locate and master specific map skill areas. Students generally like the map skill game sites. They often will focus on learning the given map skill area(s) for more extended periods of time.

Next, students can take the maps provided to them by their teacher. They should make copies of the map(s) and enlarge them if needed. The student should label the backside of each state, country, waterway, etcetera on the backside of each. Next, the student should cut out each one and make a puzzle out of the pieces.

The student can put together their map pieces like a puzzle. They should label from memory the state, country, major city, and body of water. Lastly, they can self-check their labeling from the information they labeled lightly on the reverse side.

Lastly, they may wish to color their maps. Students can work on this as often as they need to learn and retain the map skills. They can also use their additional copies to keep quizzing themselves with fresh puzzles. The map skill student-made puzzles can serve as a fun way to help students master map skills. Elementary students can learn how to make student-made games to assist them in the learning process.

★ Because You Asked

Summer will soon be here. After many discussions with my third-grade daughter, she does not wish to take any academic class over the summer. She is falling behind in her reading and reading comprehension skills. Should I let her take the summer off from academics or insist she takes classes?

Thank you for your timely question. Summer is when most students wish to take a complete break from learning and enjoy other activities. However, summertime is an ideal time for students to preserve and improve their academic skills. If your daughter is resistant to take a reading class, then ask her to commit to working an hour a day at home on her academics.

In the following chapters of this book are summertime learning activities designed to help students preserve and improve their academic skill areas. Even if she attends a reading class, she still can significantly benefit from following a summer learning plan designed to increase her skills. The proven learning techniques have helped numerous students progress in their academic areas while still having plenty of time left for family and friends.

Summer break should include learning to help all students avoid losing up to several months of their academic skills. The students will typically increase their educational skills by several months and avoid digressing in their school abilities. Summer can be fun and productive at the same time.

★ Dad's Space By David Dianis

April is the month to make sure summer teams or plans are made. The reason is that spaces may be limited and could be taken by the time school lets out.

April

Parents may wish to consider signing their son or daughter up for a team sport. There are lessons children can learn by being part of a team that is not typically learned in a classroom setting. The additional physical activity can also help students lessen their levels of academic anxiety.

Practicing a sport is a good way for parents to bond with their children while having fun themselves. Even if children are reluctant to try a team sport, they may find they like participating better than they initially thought. My daughter found after a season on a softball team that she enjoyed it more than she anticipated. She learned to perform well over time, and she became friends with students she didn't really know before. Students can learn to work together for a common goal in a team sport. The cooperative learning skills that students generally are taught while participating in a team sport can be helpful throughout their lives. Cooperative learning skills can be some of the most important ones used throughout students' lives. Happy April to all!

May

Learning Strategies To Help Students Finish
The School Year Academically Successful

May

The renewed spring air and sights of flowers bursting into bloom reminds third and fourth-grade students that school will soon conclude for the summer. The warmer days are providing numerous elementary school children with a reason to come down with spring fever. The longer days are perfect for students to spend more time outdoors with their friends.

As the school year winds down, elementary school students' schedules begin to fill up with the end of the year activities. For some students, the additional commitments can be easily added to the schedule; others will find the additional ones challenging to manage. Therefore, some special attention should be given to young students' calendars and schedules.

Every school day, grades should be checked online if available. New dues dates, assignments, tests, quizzes, and long-term projects should be added to a calendar. Students generally benefit from having a planning calendar that is a physical one, not just an electronic one. The reason is when schedules become busier, it is important that the entire family can peruse the May calendar consistently. It is important that each child or teen have their own school May calendar to avoid confusion over whose activities are for each student.

In May, students need to be extremely diligent toward their studies. Some will need to add more time to review subjects in which their grades need immediate improvement. Next, students benefit from extra reminders to help them keep up with their organizational skills. Daily cleaning of backpacks, notebooks, and folders can help students finish the school year strong.

Elementary students who find attending all of the additional end-of-the-school-year activities too taxing may need to scale back on them. Some children may need to go over their end-of-the-year schedule and select to attend the most important events. They can then eliminate the ones that may be cramming their schedule to an exhausting level. Lessening the demands of extra activities can help relieve stress and anxiety toward school. Then the third and fourth-grade students benefit from focusing on completing the school year academically strong.

The good news is numerous students who have struggled in prior months of the school year may have their academic expectations finally figured out. For some students, it can take almost the entire school year before they truly have their teacher(s) standards and curriculum understood. The heightened levels of understanding can help these types of students close out the school year on an upward note. This method can help them even more because other students may begin slowing down academically. The playing field is often more leveled out during the final months of school. Struggling students can take advantage of this scenario and use it to their advantage. When they speed up their studies while numerous others slow down, the struggling student can raise their grades to their highest they have earned all year.

★ Test-Taking Tips

As the school year comes to a close and summer is looming, students will generally see an increase in the number of tests they are given. The volume of information included on the end-of-the-year tests may expand. Therefore, third and fourth-grade students can benefit from learning and employing proven test-taking strategies.

As soon as a new unit of study is introduced in each core subject area, elementary students should begin mastering the key concept objectives. Students should play a game with a peer in their class or by themselves. The game is for the student first to review all of the bold print words, main ideas, and formulas in the unit. Next, a parent, sibling, or friend can call out one of the items listed above. Then the student can use a piece of paper, electronic device, or small whiteboard to write down as much information they can recall about the concept.

The idea is for the student to write or draw what they remember about the item to be mastered. Spelling and messier handwriting should not be a reason not to participate in the information practice game. The student can self-check their answer with their study material. Next, they should use another color to write the corrected information by their answer.

The core concepts of information should be gone over for several minutes each day. The information can also be answered orally on alternating days. The more students spend learning testable information over days generally, the easier it is to access during tests. Students also benefit from spending some time re-reading their written-out review test sheets they used to answer the called-out information.

In addition, third and fourth-grade students should be asked questions over the testable information using different wording. Numerous students are very literal during the elementary years and believe the information should be asked as it is stated in their class material. However, by the third and fourth-grade years, much of the test questions are wording somewhat differently from the information presented in the learning material. The more experience children are given having to answer practice test questions that are worded differently than they learned them, the better test-takers they often become.

Students who learn how to review and master testable information over time can become excellent test-takers. Spending time studying, writing, and or drawing the answers to testable information, the higher scores students can learn to score. Students can learn how to master the art of test-taking. Please remind the child who is reluctant to study that learning how to earn high test scores can open countless doors of opportunity throughout their life. The ability to score impressive marks on tests can lead to future scholarships and better jobs in one's life. Testing taking is a skill that can be learned even if the child has struggled with tests.

★ Quiz Taking Help

We've all heard children and teens saying *it's just a quiz*. Others say they don't need to review for quizzes. Some say I don't care about my quiz grades because they don't count for much. Also, some declare they will study for the quiz after it has already been given. Maybe we said the exact words ourselves when we were students.

However, the ability to score high quiz grades is a skill that can be taught to most students. The enormous amount of valuable points from quiz grades is almost overwhelming to think about and comprehend. Quiz grades have the power to lower or higher grades by over one letter grade per class each marking period. Students who learn early on in their journey to be educated on how to score higher quiz grades can dramatically increase their class rank and later GPAs.

First, young students may need to be taught how much their cumulated quiz grades count toward their final grade each marking period. Next, third and fourth graders benefit from learning how to prepare for announced and unannounced quizzes. Additionally, quizzes are often given in different formats than traditional tests are presented. Therefore, it is important that students learn how to prepare and stay prepared to take quizzes.

The good news is the time elementary students take to review for quizzes can count toward test review sessions. Each evening whether a quiz has been announced or not, students should go over the unit's main vocabulary words, core concepts, formulas, and primary objectives for several minutes. The review can be orally or in written form. They benefit from practicing the information in its entirety to help them retain and access it later. Also, calling out the information and possible choices can help students learn how to take quizzes that are given orally.

Next, students should practice taking matching quizzes. Students can make their own practice matching quizzes and self-check their answers. Children also benefit from a parent or sibling writing possible quiz questions on a whiteboard and answering them. This method will help because numerous quizzes are given in this format. Lastly, elementary students should be reminded that much of the test or quiz questions won't be worded exactly as they studied it. They need to analyze the question to help them determine what is the answer that most closely resembles what they learned.

Students who spend several minutes each day reviewing for announced and pop quizzes often find their grades improving. Also, the time they spend reviewing the testable information will count toward the unit test study time. Children who learn how to be great quiz and test-takers generally will have the highest grades in their academic classes. They are typically deemed to be the brightest students in the class. Therefore, it is good news that quiz and test-taking skills can be taught to those who seem to be lacking in these vital scholastic skills. Students can learn to be superior test and quiz takers.

★ Wrap-Up The School Year

As the last days of school are swiftly approaching, students will be wrapping the end of the year gifts for their teachers. They may even have the end of the year class parties and receive a fun wrapped gift from their friends or room mothers. While all the end-of-the-year parties are happening, elementary students and their parents should be collecting graded papers, quizzes, and tests from their subject areas.

The reason students and their parents should be compiling graded work from their core academic classes to serve as review information. This strategy is essential for children who are behind scholastically in one or more subject area (s). The pages will provide students with a snapshot of education skills and concepts they may need to relearn. It will also assist students when they and their parents develop a summer learning plan designed to remediate their weaker academic skills.

Students can remediate their academic issues during the summer and master skills that weren't fully mastered during the school year. The papers will clearly show core learning concepts that should be reviewed to help them retain them.

Moreover, learning builds upon itself, and numerous academic issues that students experience in the upper grades can be traced to unmastered information from their elementary years. That may seem surprising, but missing foundational knowledge can develop into learning problems in the later grades. Therefore, it is imperative that students dedicate time to relearning, reviewing, and mastering core concepts over the summer. That being said, students may think they are being asked to study their entire summer. However, most students can work forty-five minutes to an hour per day in the summer working on academics. They will find they still have plenty of time for other activities.

★ Because You Asked

> *May is the last month of the school year in our area. As summer approaches, do you have any suggestions to help my son improve his reading comprehension skills? He will be going into fifth grade and is testing behind his grade level in all of the reading comprehension school evaluations.*

Thank you for your excellent question. Over the months of summer vacation, students can significantly improve their reading comprehension skills. Your question indicates that you have important data regarding your son's reading comprehension skills. Therefore, purchase at a teacher supply store or online reading comprehension workbooks. Look for high-interest ones and are one to two months over his current reading comprehension level. Later in summer, as he improves, you will most likely need to purchase other workbooks that are again several months higher than his new, improved level. Also, look for workbooks that have stories that are one to two pages long. They should test for the main reading comprehension questions such as facts, main idea, drawing conclusions, making inferences, and analyzation skills.

Next, plan with your son a strategic plan that will have him completing three to four stories each weekday. The time can be broken up into one-story sessions. Then ask your son to pre-read the questions to the story before he reads it. After, he should read the short story three times before he answers the questions. One of the readings should be oral to help reinforce his visual and auditory comprehension skills. On the final reading, he should begin to locate the answers to the questions he hasn't yet found.

Then he should answer the reading comprehension questions. He should look through the story and underline the answers in the written text. This method will help remediate his skills by having him prove his answers in the written story. This technique can help end students' tendency to guess and just mark answers. Next, a parent or older sibling should check his answers. Please have him locate the definition of any word he can't accurately define himself. Most workbooks will include the answers in the back of the book. The person checking should mark all of the correct and incorrect answers and give a percentage grade.

If your son scores below seventy percent on three to four stories, then the level may be too high, and he should begin again at an easier level. He can then work his way back up to the current workbook. Each incorrect answer should be gone over with him. Then he should relocate the answer in the text. Over time students generally, find they are enjoying reading the high-interest stories and learning from them. In addition, the questions are typically designed to strengthen the different types of reading comprehension skill areas.

As your child begins to score over eighty-five percent on ten or more stories, he should probably be moved up to the next level. Over the summer, students can overcome their reading comprehension issues and make substantial improvements.

★ Mom's Space By Karen Dianis

At the end of each school year, children often feel the excitement over finishing another part of their educational journey. As the school winds down and dreams of summer vacation loom in children's minds, some end-of-the-year discussions can significantly assist students.

After school is out, have a discussion regarding the school year with each of my children. Talk about and write down the high points of the year. Even children who claim to dislike school can typically come up with positive aspects of the academic year. Parents may need to prompt their children and help them think of at least ten good items from the school year.

Next, talk about the negative parts of the academic school year. Try to limit the list to the top ten unless there are more issues that should be addressed. Write them down as well. Then talk about how the negative items on their list can become positives during the upcoming school year. If there are any items on the negative list that you feel need to be addressed by a school counselor or expert, they may need to be checked out; please make an appointment with the school to go over the areas of concern.

Then brainstorm ways that the negative items may be remediated or worked on to help transform them. Struggling students can benefit from the idea that problems can be worked on and eventually overcome. They also may find solace in the fact that most people will have to overcome obstacles in their lives.

Then discuss ways that you have personally faced obstacles and overcome them in your life. You may want to ask family members to do the same. Children can benefit from understanding that issues happen in almost everyone's life, and typically they can be overcome or lessened in their effects.

The discussion should then end on a positive note. Students may want to make a collage to demonstrate the good and bad points of their school year. Then they may want to make another collage to show ways they are going to use to help themselves overcome some of their challenges.

Remember, attitude does affect one's ability to perform in school, according to brain science. If students learn, they can work toward overcoming academic school issues; they may find they have a better attitude toward learning. Children can also benefit from every morning before school to declare several positive words about themselves and their upcoming school day. This strategy can assist struggling students to continue to view themselves as capable and intelligent students. It can also help bring a more positive tone toward learning and their school day. When students focus more on the positives and less on the negative parts of the school, they may surprise themselves and find the scholastic success they once deemed impossible for them to attain. Remember that a more positive person generally can attract more positive situations and people to their lives. Happy May to all.

June

Summer Brain Drain Prevention

The school bells will soon be ringing for the last time. Excited third and fourth graders will be rushing out the school doors. Cheers will be heard as papers are fluttering high into the air, as they almost touch the sky. Happy children with broad smiles are ready for some time away from school. The more relaxed days of summer filled with friends and family are on children's minds.

As students exit the building, the sights and sounds of summer are everywhere one looks. Freedom from the daily school schedule is now here for young children. As students rush home with thoughts of how they will spend the summer. As children board the busses, they can be heard chanting; *school is out.*

Typically, young children's thoughts are wandering farther and farther away from academics. Summer sports, crafts, trips, and playtime fill elementary students' minds with bubbling excitement. Another year is now over. In children's minds, it may seem like decades before the new one begins.

Numerous students' minds wander further from academics as the busses pull away for the final time of the year. Others may begin to realize that they will be spending some time on learning. The good news is that third and fourth graders can have a fun summer while still growing their academic skills. They can also prevent the dreaded summer brain drain from occurring by spending several hours a week relearning, reviewing, and mastering core school concepts.

Children struggling in one or more academic skill areas should spend an hour a day working on bolstering their scholastic skills. Elementary-age students performing at the average levels should work approximately forty-five minutes a day to improve their educational skills. Third and fourth-grade students performing at the top quartile of their peers in their academics should also prevent the summer brain drain. High academically achieving students benefit from spending thirty minutes a day on academics. This summer schedule will help them prevent summer learning loss.

Remember, summer learning loss is a proven idea. Students who don't crack a book or engage in any type of learning activities over the summer generally lose up to three months of their academic gains. That is losing almost one-third of the school year's achievement. Also, students can benefit from keeping their scholastic learning going forward. Students can gain as much as one year of academic progress during the summer.

★ Plan Learning Time Each Weekday

Summertime is a wonderful time for students to jump ahead in their academic skills while having plenty of time leftover. If a student balks about dedicating thirty minutes to an hour a day to summer learning, this next idea may help. There are 168 hours in a week. If a student spends 5 hours a week learning, that will leave 163 hours leftover for other activities.

Students may wish to break their summer learning sessions up into fifteen- or twenty-minute intervals. Others may want to do their entire learning time at one large chunk. Either way can work for young children to keep growing in their scholastic skills. Some third and fourth graders may want to alternate between learning schedules.

At the beginning of the summer, as soon as school lets out, students should begin their summer learning program. The reason is that if students take a break from learning, they will often not start a remedial or scholastic growing program. The longer the daily program is put off, the more likely it will be forgotten about and not implemented.

★ Fun Ways To Continue Learning And Reading In The Summer

Reading for fun can be a foreign idea for students who have struggled or demonstrating reading problems. The summertime is an idea for elementary-age students to choose age and reading level appropriate reading material of high interest. The public library is an excellent resource for students to be able to choose the books they want to read. Allowing young readers to choose the books they want to read can help inspire them to read.

The library books generally are classified by the library into reading levels, or the librarian can provide that information to the student. Reading books should be chosen that are two months above their current reading level. If the student wants to read some books that read just below or above their level, they can still improve their skills by reading them.

The public library typically offers reading comprehension tests or quizzes that are taken online to help improve comprehension skills. The reading comprehension quizzes or tests can be taken within several days after they finished the book. Students may benefit from earning points for every book they read. They also may be motivated to read the material carefully if they are given points for each reading comprehension test they pass. The points can count toward rewards for their efforts. Again, the rewards don't have to monetary based. The rewards can be family game time, movie night, or a week without chores.

Before the reading program begins, students and a parent should determine the number of books that should be read over the summer. There can be a category for shorter books and one for chapter books. The number of books should be determined by the idea that a child should read for twenty to thirty minutes a day or more. The child's reading level, pace, and fluency should be taken into account. Setting reading goals and checking several times a week that they are being met will help keep the reading program from falling to the wayside.

As students begin a new short story or chapter book, they should peruse the reading material to help them determine more about the content. Next, they should have a dictionary or electronic device to look up words they are unfamiliar with or can't decode. Young students benefit from reading with a parent, friend, babysitter, or sibling. Reading aloud will help improve children's fluency levels. It also helps keep students more focused and concentrated during the reading sessions.

Some reading-challenged students may want to read a page, and then the other person reading with them reads a page and so on. This method helps struggling readers become less burdened by reading sessions. If they can take turns, they often feel more motivated to read. Young students can grow their reading and comprehension skills over the summer. Students can learn to be excellent readers.

★ Summer Reading Decoding And Blending Skills Improvement

Students of all reading levels can improve their decoding and blending skills over the summer. One helpful way to help young students progress in their reading skills is to add seven to twelve new words a week to their daily learning time. The words should be ones they have yet to master or ones that will be included in their upcoming year's curriculum. The words should be what I refer to as high-use words. This definition means there are words students in their grade level they really need to know because of the high frequency of use.

Lists of words that are frequently used in each grade level curriculum are available online, or the local public school typically has them. Next, students benefit from making a flashcard with each new word. The word should be written on one side, and the phonetic spelling and definition on the reverse side. Students with reading issues can benefit from color-coding the word. The vowel spelling and any affixes should be highlighted in the same color. This technique helps students' ability to blend and decode multi-syllable words.

Each day third and fourth grades should read each of the words on their to-be-learned list. They should read the words at least seven times each day. If the student struggles with one or more of their new words, they should repeat the word with a parent or older sibling ten times to help bring in more repetition. Next, they should orally spell the word while writing it on paper. This strategy will help students master words more quickly.

At the end of each week, the words the student has already learned from past weeks should be reviewed. The weekly review of the previous weeks' words helps students retain and master them. Then students should look for sentences when they are reading that contain the words from their weekly lists. Students can make a game out of locating their new reading words. Children should give themselves points for every sentence they locate that contains one or more of their reading words.

Over the summer, students can add an additional hundred or more words to their reading is known word lists. This method will help them improve their skills. It will also help teach them more phonetic rules and affixes. In addition, they will learn how to decode and blend multi-syllable words. Lastly, they can also improve their spelling skills by learning how to spell the words by working with them over the summer.

This technique can vastly improve students' reading skills over the summer without bogging them down with hours of formalized instruction. It can also help restore their academic self-esteem. Students can learn how to reach reading goals over the summer. They can also learn how to restore or gain a scholastic edge prior to the new school year starting up again.

★ Grammar Fun

Modern schools have often scaled down the amount of academic time set aside to teach grammar skills. However, possessing impressive grammar skills can help students throughout their lives. Numerous students will find that having excellent grammar skills can lead them to future scholastic opportunities, scholarships, and job promotions.

In the summer, elementary students can learn grammar concepts. Others can reinforce and review their grammar skills while having fun. Young children can play the game *Grammar Acting Out, which can be a fun* way to work on grammar.

One child, teen, or adult can call out a noun, pronoun, verb, adjective, adverb, preposition, conjunction, or interjection. The other student or children can act out an example of the part of speech called out. Then the person calling out the part of speech can try to guess each child's actions to determine what the object or description word is being acted out. Even colors can be demonstrated by children finding an object representing the color.

Then the person who is calling out the parts of speech can ask the other players to help him, or her guess what each child's acting out demonstrating. The person who is able to obtain the most correct guesses will receive a point. Next, another part of speech to be acted out is called out. As the part of speech is called out, the group can orally define the part of speech. An example of this is a noun is a *person, place, thing, idea, or feeling.* This game can provide young elementary-age children with hours of fun while learning or reviewing the eight parts of speech. The acting out will give students who are kinesthetic learners additional reinforcement. Kinesthetic learners are ones that learn at their optimum level through actions or movement.

Throughout the summer, students can employ fun ways to learn or reinforce grammar skills. They typically can learn how to understand, remember and master grammar concepts while having a fun time. By the end of the summer, most children will have mastered the eight parts of speech if they play this game on a consistent basis. By the time school resumes, elementary students can be ahead of the game by mastering the eight parts of speech.

★ Daily Math Improvement

STEM classes have become the focus of most school curriculums throughout the world. Therefore, elementary students will benefit from practicing math skills. Students should work on retaining, remediating, and pre-learning math throughout the weeks of summer.

Children benefit from working on three to four math problems five days a week. They should work on problems that review operations they learned during the previous school year. Consistent review of math formulas helps students from regressing in their skills.

The grade-level math problems can be found online or from workbooks from a teacher supply store. Elementary students who are behind in their math skills can work on remediating their skills during the summer. Struggling math students can catch up on their math skills and fill in math gaps before the upcoming school year.

Students benefit from working out the math problems using colored pencils to increase their interest and visual stimulus. Each step of the problem should be worked out with a different colored pencil. For instance, when the student is to borrow or carry, a selected color should be used. Another color should be used for adding, subtracting, multiplying, or dividing operations. Then students benefit from working the problem in reverse to help them self-check their work. They can self-correct mistakes they may have made.

Students who work on working three to four mathematical problems a day during the summer can grow their skills up to a year. Elementary-age students can avoid future math pitfalls by closing math gaps they may have developed. Mathematical operations build upon ones taught in earlier grades. Therefore, it is imperative that math concepts be mastered at every grade level.

As the summer progresses, students benefit from pre-learning new mathematical concepts and operations that will be taught in their upcoming grade level. The following grade-level math formulas can be found seeking out online math-free math sites. They can generally be found on their school's curriculum website.

Elementary students who pre-learn some of the math operations and formulas can find better academic success in the next school year. By working on three to four mathematical procedures each weekday, students can learn to have fantastic math skills.

★ Fun Written Language Skills Improvement

Children enjoy receiving and reading postcards from interesting places. The pictures on the front can be enchanting representations of the beauty found in the world. Students can have fun designing their own postcards from phone pictures, magazines, drawings, etcetera. They can create their own fabulous places or ones they would like to visit.

June

On the reverse side, students can improve their written language skills by writing notes to family members, friends, or people they would like to meet. The messages can include details about the place they created or factual information about their picture. Children can write sentences describing fun activities they are doing or going to do. Next, elementary students should add impressive adjectives and adverbs to paint a mental picture for the reader. Then they can edit their sentences for correct punctuation. Students can also ask a parent, friend, or older sibling to help them edit their notes.

The editing process of rewriting sentences to make them more interesting can help improve children's written language skills. Students may want to pre-write their postcard notes on other paper or an electronic device prior to copying them on the backside of their postcard. This method will help students do a better job editing their work. They may want to have a contest with themselves to make each postcard note more creative than the last one.

The postcards can be placed in a memory book for students. This activity can also include real postcards from places they visit during the summer. Even local trips to museums may be included in their memory postcard writing activity.

Students may wish to write postcards to friends and relatives who live in different places and have them write back. This activity can include writing and receiving postcards from numerous cities or countries. Most children will really enjoy receiving postcards from others in the family or friends.

Elementary-age students can learn how to improve their written language skills while creating lasting memories. They benefit from changing common nouns and verbs for synonyms that are more impressive to read. Their sentences can include ones that are simple, compound, and complex. Over the summer, students should aim to write one postcard note per week. The creative writing activity can help keep students from digressing in their written language skills. Third and fourth grades can grow their written language skills while having fun and creating lasting memories.

★ Science Made Fun

As we all know, science has become a class that has increased in emphasis in the last decade. The STEM classes have become the main focus of numerous curriculums because business has demanded it. Over the summer, young students can gain an academic edge in their ability to learn and master core science concepts.

Children can perform safe and fun scientific activities each week. The science grade-level experiments can be ones that use items found in most homes. Some may require a few ingredients to be purchased from a local store. The grade-level safe experiments can be found on teacher sites online, or in science workbooks found at teacher supply stores. Students benefit from performing science learning experiments with a parent weekly. Each step of the experiment should be gone over very carefully. The desired outcome should be reviewed before the experiment is started. Next, the experiment and what science concept(s) it teaches should be explained by a parent.

Then the experiment should be conducted with all safety precautions taken. The child should write up the results and notes about what the experiment taught. Next, if the results didn't happen as expected, then each step of the experiment should be gone over to locate the mistake. Some of the science experiments can create fun and cool ways to learn the upcoming grade-level concepts. They can also review the past grade-level concepts that haven't been mastered or need review.

In addition, the experiments can make learning science concepts fun and exciting. Students will also learn about following step-by-step procedures to create an expected outcome. Children may also find a new interest in science. The visual learning the experiments provide will also help students to retain new scientific concepts.

★ Fabulous Fridays

Fridays are numerous people's favorite day of the week. During the summertime, third and fourth grades can benefit from *Fabulous Fridays*. On Fridays, students can choose what learning activity they wish to do instead of their regular learning routine. The *Fabulous Fridays'* choices can include playing board games with friends that include numeration procedures such as counting play money. Making change with play money which is part of countless board games, can help increase mastery of math facts. The addition and subtraction required for board games is a wonderful way for students to progress in math.

Students may wish to choose to play learning bingo which can be found online or in most teacher supply stores. The subject area of the bingo game can be located in almost every subject area and grade level.

If the student likes sports, then they can choose to keep score for a professional baseball or soccer game. The scorekeeping should include research on statistics on players and teams. They can also calculate where the team stands in relation to the first and last place, etcetera. They can calculate player averages. If there isn't a game until the weekend, then they can postpone the activity until later.

Map skills and geography concepts can also be practiced by putting puzzles together. Students can also play free online games to help them master these skills. Students may believe that geography and map skills are unimportant to know. However, as they continue to journey through the grade levels, map skills will often count for a tremendous amount of points in various classes.

Students may wish to decide what fun type of learning games they want to play on Fabulous Fridays. There are numerous learning games that can be found online or at teacher supply stores that reinforce spelling and reading skills. When students are having fun learning generally, they are more focused and more engaged in the learning process. Children can progress in their academic skills while having fun playing learning games.

★ Because You Asked

> *My son just completed the third grade. His end-of-the-year testing indicates that he is almost a grade level behind in most of his academic classes. He wants to wait until mid-July to begin an at-home remediation program. Should he be allowed to take a five-week break for academic learning? Can he catch up this summer and be closer to the fourth-grade level in his skills?*

Thank you for your questions. Most parents can relate to their children's wish for time away from educational learning in the summer and desire to take a break from learning. It is easy to give in to children and put off remedial education for several weeks or a month or more. However, if your son is performing behind in one or more academic skill areas, then he should begin an at-home remedial program as soon as school concludes for the year. The reason is it can take several months of remediation activities and learning exercises to help bring his skills closer to his current grade-level standards.

A child who is performing six months to a year or more behind his or her current grade-level expectations should work on their scholastic learning for at least an hour a day in the summer. Numerous students benefit from working on remediation for several hours a day to help catch them up. The learning time can be divided into smaller segments to help students focus on their learning activities.

Remedial learning activities can include learning games and educational crafts such as making parts of speech collages. Writing postcards which are described in this month, is also an effective way to reinforce written language skills. Children generally learn more when they are enjoying the learning process. The additional remediation should be divided into twenty to thirty-minute segments per scholastic core class per weekday.

Over the summer, consistent learning sessions can help students close learning gaps. Children can grow their learning skills by months and even a year or more. Students could find themselves beginning the school year on grade level or just below if they were significantly behind. Others will start the school year off academically, functioning above their current grade-level standards. Students can remediate low functioning scholastic areas while still having fun in the summer. They will also be able to have plenty of time to enjoy other activities.

★ Dad's Space By Dave Dianis

The month of June is an ideal time to emphasize teachable moments in everyday situations. When I took my children to a ball game, concert or event, I would discuss with them several ideas. First, how much the adult and child ticket prices were. Next, how many children and adults were in attendance. Then we would estimate the amount of money the event, game, or movie theater was taking in. Next, if there were a concession stand where we were, we would estimate the amount of a particular item we thought it was selling that day. Next, my children and I would estimate the potential profit and subtract the possible cost per item to the seller.

These types of teachable moments help teach my children math skills and many other valuable lessons. My children and their friends enjoyed the calculation process. Then we would check our calculations with a calculator for accuracy. Happy June to all!

July

Summer Fun Learning

July

The site of flags and firework posters in stores remind people that July is arriving with a bang. Warmer days, sounds of splashing, and laughter fill children with delight. They know that the entire month of July is dedicated to summertime. Baseball bats and soccer balls are a common sight around the neighborhoods. Children can be seen darting to friends' homes and biking up the streets. The month of July brings fun and excitement to children as they continue to celebrate the days of summer.

In July, third and fourth-grade children benefit from continuing their summer learning plan designed to help them achieve higher grades in their fall classes. If a student hasn't begun a summer learning plan, then they should start one.

The summer brain drain is preventable. Students who spend time each day learning and reviewing core concepts can significantly benefit from their efforts. In July, students benefit from working for an hour to an hour and a half each weekday on academics is all it takes. Reading for improvement time should be included in the daily lessons.

Students can learn to have fun learning while still having plenty of time left for other activities. They will benefit from beginning the school year with a restored or preserved scholastic edge. In addition, they can find themselves educationally ahead of their peers at the beginning months of the school year. Even if a student struggled in the past school year(s), they can close their learning gaps and become academically successful students.

★ Splash Spelling

July is the perfect time for students to continue working on improving and strengthening their spelling skills. Splash spelling can be a very fun way to learn how to spell words students have yet to master. Children who enjoy water or water sports can benefit from playing *Splash Spelling*.

Splash Spelling can be played in the water with adult supervision or on dry land. Students will need a beach ball and a list of words to be learned how to spell. *Splash Spelling* can be played with two or more players. First, students should go over a pre-made list of ten to twenty words to learn. The words should be tailored made for their specific spelling needs. The words should be ones they haven't mastered from the previous school year and ones from the next school year's online lists. The online lists for the upcoming school year can be readily found on curriculum sites. Also, spelling workbooks can be a fantastic resource. They can be purchased from teacher supply stores or online.

Next, comprise a list of ten to twenty words with a mixture of the previous school year's spelling words that need to be reviewed. The remainder of the words should be from the upcoming school year's curriculum list. The school website your son or daughter is enrolled in may also offer a list of spelling words. The words can also be from word lists of their upcoming grade level should master. These grade-level mastery lists can be found online.

Then go over the words and their spellings with the players of *Splash Spelling*. Allow each player to review the list for several minutes. Next, bounce the beach ball around to each player, trying to keep it in the air to music. When the music stops, then whoever has the beach ball is given the word off the list to spell. If they are in a pool or on land, they can jump up and down as they spell the word. Children who are land lovers can pretend they are in the water bobbing up and down while spelling the word they are given.

When a player can have two tries to spell the word correctly. If the player spells the word correctly on the first try, they receive 2 points. Suppose it takes the second try to spell a word correctly, then they should be given a point. When a student misspells the word twice, then the other players should review the spelling with the player. The word should be kept on the list instead of checked off to keep the game going. This game will also provide additional spelling words reinforcement.

When players master their current list of spelling words to 80% or better, then the mastered words should be changed to new ones to be learned. The process should be repeated until students learn to spell a minimum of 100 words during the summer.

Splash Spelling Game can be played on land throughout the school year. It is a fun way to help students learn their grade level's weekly spelling words. The more active students may find they are able to focus on learning their spelling words for more extended periods of time. *Splash Spelling* can help learning spelling words become a source of fun instead of boredom. Spelling-challenged students can learn to be excellent spellers.

July

★ July History Fun For Written Language Improvement

Color shades of red, white, and blue fill the nation's stores and peoples' homes. The Fourth of July is now here. Third and fourth graders are curious about the Revolutionary War that brought independence to the United States.

Therefore, July is an ideal time for third and fourth graders to learn about one or more key people from the War of Independence. Elementary students can choose an American patriot they want to research and write a several hundred-word report about for an interesting essay. This idea can become a family activity where each member chooses a patriot to write about and present their information to the entire family.

First, each child or adult should choose one or more patriots to research. A list of essential patriots can be found online or at a public library. Next, each child and adult should read online sources and public library books to help them research their selected people. Each participant should use a minimum of two historical sources for their written report.

Third and fourth graders can write about their chosen patriot's significance to the American Revolution, earlier background, family, and life after the war. They may want to include details about the patriot's favorite food, hobby, or fun personal facts. In addition, the report should consist of what significant impact the patriot still has in today's society because of their contributions. Lastly, if there are any monuments, statues, coins, or remembrance of them exists.

Next, third and fourth graders can write a short report to share with their families about their chosen patriot. The report should be a minimum of a page and a half in length. Then the third and fourth graders may want to make drawings or a collage of items that relate to the patriot they researched. The collage or graphics can be added to their report. The reports can be a very fun way for family members to learn about and share research about significant people from the Revolutionary War and the founding of the United States. The patriot reports can be an enjoyable way to spark an interest in history, politics, government, and writing.

The participation from other family members can demonstrate to children the importance of being lifelong learners. It can also be a fabulous way to learn history together and keep the meaning in the Fourth of July. This activity can be repeated each summer to create lasting memories while learning about history, presenting information to others, and improving writing skills. Students can have fun while learning with their families!

★ July Reading Improvement

Reading improvement can alter a student's life in various ways. The benefits of possessing excellent reading skills are numerous in one's life. Third and fourth graders can increase their reading skills while learning interesting and useful information. In July, children can read about interesting places, inventions, historical people, scientific discoveries, or other areas of appropriate high interest.

The student should choose the books to be read to improve reading skills. When students read books, they enjoy their ability to focus on what they are reading generally increases. Students may find they enjoy reading more and are willing to spend additional time reading each day. Third and fourth graders may want to have a contest with other family members or friends to reach reading goals. Students can set reading goals such as how many books or pages read. How much time they read each day is another goal to work toward throughout the remainder of the summer.

Each goal that is reached, the student should be rewarded with a predetermined privilege or reasonable item. The reward system can help inspire even the most reluctant readers to want to read to improve their skills.

As students read, they should work on blending and decoding each word they come across that they aren't familiar with or haven't mastered. Then they should make a running reading list of all of the words they need to work on in order to read instantly.

Students who have to describe the words jumping around on the page should read with a marker that covers the entire page. In the middle of the marker, an adult can cut a rectangle large enough to allow one multisyllable word at a time to be read. This technique will help stop the words from jumping around on the page because only one word at a time will be visible. As students master seeing and reading one word at a time, then they can add another word and so on. Over time students with reading issues such as Dyslexia can find they are able to read a page without the words moving around on the page for them. This technique can help Dyslexic students learn better methods to help them read independently. It can also help students with focusing issues concentrate on reading the words, not just skimming over them. Students with diagnosed reading problems can learn how to overcome them.

★ July Cooking For Math Improvement And Increasing Planning Skills

Holiday-themed cooking can be a tremendous way to help students improve their math skills. It can also teach them organizational planning as an added benefit. Children typically enjoy helping prepare memorable holiday-themed foods. Third and fourth graders may wish to choose a holiday food to help make for family and friends. They can find numerous choices of kid-friendly holiday recipes online or in cookbooks designed for children.

Next, children can take inventory of the ingredients that their family already has. Then they can make a grocery list of the needed items. Then they can look up online or go to the store with a family member and calculate the amount of money each item costs. Next, they can add up the entire cost of each recipe to make. The column addition can be done in amounts of three. Students can add the cost of three items and then add up the total of all of the totals in each group of three.

Students can then practice subtracting by using an amount of money, such as twenty or fifty dollars, from the total cost of the recipe to be made. If there are several of the same items, they can use multiplication skills to help them determine the cost of the identical items.

Next, planning skills can be improved by a parent assisting their child in organizing the materials needed to make the recipe. Also, the preparation and cooking time can be planned. The number of servings can also be planned out in advance. Any other particular directions can be planned for too. A parent or adult will need to assist the child f the oven or stove is required to prepare the recipe.

Holiday cooking can be a fun way to improve a child's math and planning skills while having fun. Most children also feel a sense of accomplishment when they serve a holiday recipe to family and friends they helped prepare and plan. Children can learn math and planning skills while having fun! Children can learn from everyday activities.

Learning how to succeed scholastically can be fun and effective!

Grade Transformer for the Modern Student

★ Parents' Space By Karen And Dave Dianis

It is easy for children who have struggled in school to feel they will always face scholastic difficulties. Negative emotions and thoughts can significantly impact children's ability to view themselves as academically successful students. Fear of certain classes can prevent some students from enjoying the process of learning. It can also lower students' educational self-esteem.

The good news is that proactive parents can help transform their student's attitudes toward school or specific areas of study. For example, in July, a parent or both parents can talk to their child about the previous school years and areas of academic weaknesses.

Please discuss with your third or fourth grader openly and honestly the areas of academic troubles they demonstrated in the past grade levels. Then go over the strategies they have been employing during the summer to overcome them. Point out that each new school year is a fresh start. Also, bring up the concept that they can learn to excel in the same areas that have been troublesome to them.

Next, go over any weaker scholastic area that may need to be given more time during the remaining weeks of summer. Additionally, help them understand that they will begin the school year implementing a proactive remediation plan to help them learn how to excel in areas they once demonstrated difficulty learning.

In addition, go over the attitude that will best serve them they should demonstrate to their teacher(s). Please remind your child that you are there to help them. Also, remind your child that a positive attitude can help them perform better in their classes. A cheerful disposition can also affect their teacher's view of them. Students with a negative attitude may find themselves given less assistance in class and possibly score lower grades. Help your child understand these complex ideas before a new school year starts to help it be a more academically successful and happier one. Positive and winning attitudes can help raise your child's grades and likeability.

★ Because You Asked

How important is writing down assignments to a child's academic performance if they struggle to be organized?

July

Thank you for your excellent question. In today's electronic world, one could say that writing down assignments has become obsolete. However, in my professional opinion, children benefit from writing down their assignments, daily tasks, and activities to help promote organizational skills. After each assignment, task and activity are completed each day; the task should be checked off as done.

Children and teens typically enjoy checking off assignments, tasks, and activities as completed. This also helps them develop time management skills along with organizational skills. It also provides children with visual feedback on what they have to manage each day. This strategy will also benefit your child by helping him or her complete more of their daily schedule.

In July, children should practice writing down their daily study assignments, tasks, i.e., chores and activities. The act of writing down and keeping track of the day's schedule will help students increase their accountability levels. The summer is an ideal time to help children learn how to keep a daily record of their schedule. In addition, it will assist students who have difficulty writing down items on a calendar or paper to improve their skills. The more children can do in the summer to help them improve their paper-pencil skills, the better the outcome for the upcoming school year can be.

Students can learn how to have effective organizational skills and improve their time management skills during the summer. Children can learn to become better at task completion and increase their responsibility skills. They also can have plenty of time to do activities they enjoy with their family and friends. The earlier children learn to be organized; they will generally benefit from earning higher grades by applying good organizational strategies.

Bibliography

The American Heritage Dictionary of the English Language, 4th ed., Texas: Houghton Mifflin in Company, 2004

Ames, Louise Bates. Is Your Child in the Wrong Grade? Pennsylvania: Modern Learning Press, 1978.

Armstrong, T. Multiple Intelligence in the Classroom. Virginia: Association for Supervision and Curriculum Development, 1994.

Butler, Kathleen. It's All in Your Mind: A Student's Guide to Learning Style. Connecticut: The Learner's Dimension, 1988

Capehart, Jody, and Paul Warren. You and You're A.D.D. Child. Tennessee: Thomas Nelson, Inc., 1995.

Dianis, Barbara. Don't Count Me Out! A Guide to Better Grades and Test Scores Pre K-12Th Making Winners Out of Struggling Students, despite Dyslexia, ADD/ADHD, or Educational Difficulties., North Carolina: Lulu Publishing Company, 2013

Druckman, D. & Swet, J. Enhancing Human Performance: Issues, Theories, and Techniques. Washington D.C. National Academy Press, 1988.

Erlauer, Laura. The Brain-Compatible Classroom. Virginia: Association for Supervision and Curriculum Development, 2003.

Learner, Janet. Learning Disabilities Theories, Diagnosis, and Teaching Strategies. 3rd ed.Texas: Houghton Mifflin in Company, 1981.

Bibliography

Salvia, John, and James E. Ysseldyke. Assessment in Special and Remedial Education 3rd ed. Texas: Houghton Mifflin in Company, 1985

Satter, Jerome M. Assessment of Children's Intelligence and Special Abilities. 2nd. Ed. Massachusetts: Allyn and Bacon, Inc.,1982

Webster's New College Dictionary, 3rd ed. New York: Macmillian, 1997

Glossary of Terms

Attention Deficit Disorder ADD: "Attention Deficit Disorder is a biologically based condition causing a persistent pattern of difficulties resulting in one or more of the following: inattention, organizational problems, focusing problems, impulsivity, hyperactivity or hypoactivity."

Inattention: is characterized by difficulty attending or focusing on a specific task. "Students with Attention Deficit Disorder often become distracted within a matter of a few minutes." Inattentive behavior may also cause problems with staying focused on tasks and in the area of organization. Students with Inattention may lose their belongings and experience difficulties keeping track of papers, books, and assignments. Turning in work is often a problem for these students as well as" keeping track of time, completing tasks, "and these students often "make careless errors."

Attention Deficit Hyperactivity Disorder ADHD: is characterized by difficulty inhibiting behavior. "These students are in constant motion. During classroom instruction, they may engage in excessive fiddling, have problems staying seated or squirm in their chair."

Impulsivity: is characterized by difficulty in controlling impulses. "These students often do not stop and think before they act. They may say and do whatever comes into their mind without thinking about the consequences. These students might say something inappropriate and regret it later, blurt out

Glossary of Terms

a response to question before a person is done speaking to them," or have they experience difficulty waiting in line and waiting for their turn.

ADD or ADHD—The difference between ADD and ADHD is: "Clinically, the term ADHD stands for Attention Deficit Hyperactivity Disorder. A person may either be diagnosed with ADHD or ADD, depending on whether they are hyperactive or not. It is possible for someone to have ADD without being hyperactive. ADD, and ADHD often result in learning problems, organizational issues, and various types of behavior problems."

Auditory Learners: "are learners whose optimum learning takes place by taking in information through hearing."

Dyscalculia: "is the lack of ability to perform mathematical functions."

Dysgraphia: "is characterized by extremely poor handwriting or the inability to perform the motor movement required for handwriting."

Dyslexia: "is characterized by the impairment of the ability to read. It often leads to learning problems in the areas of reading, reading comprehension, spelling, written language and grammar."

Kinesthetic Learner: "are learners whose optimum learning takes place when information is taken in through the senses."

Learning Difference: "is a disorder in which there is an educationally significant discrepancy between estimated intellectual potential and actual level of performance."

Struggling Student: is any student performing below grade level requirements or not at the optimum level for their intellectual level of ability in one or more subject areas.

Visual Learner: "are learners whose optimum learning takes place through the information that is taken in through sight."

About the Author

Barbara Dianis earned a Master of Education Degree, Special Education Pre-K-12th, Language Learning Disabilities, and Psychometry. She also has a double BA in Elementary Education and Learning Disabilities. Dianis has taught Struggling, Dyslexia, ADD/ADHD, and Language Learning challenged students how to succeed scholastically in school. Dianis has authored *Don't Count Me Out!*, other *Grade Transformer for the Modern Student Editions,* and educational articles in popular media outlets, been a guest on radio stations throughout the United States, Canada, and 55 other countries, and appeared on TV as an educational expert.

www.ingramcontent.com/pod-product-compliance
Lightning Source LLC
Chambersburg PA
CBHW071859070526
44583CB00016B/1760